School Climate and Culture vis-à-vis Student Learning

School Climate and Culture vis-à-vis Student Learning

Keys to Collaborative Problem Solving and Responsibility

Cletus R. Bulach, Fred C. Lunenburg,
and Les Potter

ROWMAN & LITTLEFIELD
Lanham • Boulder • New York • London

Published by Rowman & Littlefield
A wholly owned subsidary of The Rowman & Littlefield Publishing Group, Inc.
4501 Forbes Boulevard, Suite 200, Lanham, Maryland 20706
www.rowman.com

Unit A, Whitacre Mews, 26-34 Stannary Street, London SE11 4AB

British Library Cataloguing in Publication Information Available

Library of Congress Cataloging-in-Publication Data
978-1-4758-2922-8 (cloth)
978-1-4758-2923-5 (paper)
978-1-4758-2924-2 (electronic)

∞™ The paper used in this publication meets the minimum requirements of American National Standard for Information Sciences—Permanence of Paper for Printed Library Materials, ANSI/NISO Z39.48-1992.

Printed in the United States of America

Contents

Preface

PURPOSE OF THE BOOK

A November 2015 report by the National Center for Education Evaluation and Regional Assistance compared the progress of underperforming students assigned to a reading intervention with the progress of students who were not assigned to an intervention. The students assigned to the intervention had lower scores than those who were not assigned to an intervention. The cost for this intervention or reform that lasted between March 2008 and the present was $14,204,399. This is the most recent example of a school reform that did not work.

The purpose of our book is to describe a reform that improves test scores, reduces dropouts, and decreases bullying behavior. Before we do that, let us look at some other reports on school reform. There is the report by the National Center on Education and the Economy (2007) that called for a comprehensive school reform. The report stated that there is a growing mismatch between the type of students our schools are producing and the needs of the economy. The World Wide Web has over 10 pages of titles on school reform.

The initiative for school reform is a national effort and is spearheaded by an organization called the School Reform Initiative based in Denver, Colorado. A recent 2012 publication by Balfanz, Bridgeland, Bruce, and Fox described improvements in dropout prevention and graduation rates as a result of school reform. While there are many calls for school reform, there has been little, if any, progress in improving our schools.

In a 2015 report about school improvement grants (SIG) for large city schools, US Department of Education secretary Arne Duncan reported progress but also concluded the following:

However, it should be noted that performance in these SIG schools continued to be low even after three years of intervention and support. In fact, on average, the percentage of students who were proficient and above in these schools after three years of the program remained below eligible schools that were not funded. It was also discouraging to note that performance gains leveled off after three years at relatively low levels. (p 43)

While there are many initiatives and suggestions on school reform, there is no approach that addresses the six areas needed for a comprehensive reform. These six areas are the following: discipline, basic needs of humans, culture and climate, control, parent and community involvement, and levels of openness and trust. Discipline is one of the main problems in classrooms across the United States. Colombi and Osher (2015) wrote that the institution of successful discipline practices has not occurred. They indicated that school officials have to change disciplinary practices in order to improve school climate and student achievement.

Time lost to the instructional process because teachers have to stop teaching and discipline students is addressed in chapter 1. Many teachers lose 30 days of instruction each year because of discipline problems. The culture and climate are not positive in many schools and are even toxic in some schools, leading to poor motivation and not enough time on task. Each chapter in the book addresses this crucial need.

Control is a key area. Our schools have to be a highly controlled environment in order for students and faculty to feel safe. Consequently, the administration and faculty have to be in control. This can create a problem. The more a person feels controlled, the more he or she is likely to resist that control. School officials need to learn how to give control to subordinates without giving it up. Having some control over what happens to a person is one of life's five basic needs. If a person has no control over what is happening, resistance and lack of motivation are the result. Gray (2009) stated that our schools are a prison, because students are controlled, causing students to dislike going to school.

This lack of motivation causes low test scores and discipline problems. In this book we describe how to give control to faculty and students without giving it up. Control always involves some form or power and there are only nine forms of power. Chapter 4 describes the nine forms of power. Five forms are freeing forms that give control without giving it up. Four forms are controlling forms that are used when the freeing forms do not work.

Parent and community involvement in the schools is somewhat effective at the elementary school level, but is lacking in grades 4–12. This creates a situation where teachers are trying to improve student behavior and affect a change for 6 hours a day and 180 days a year. The remaining 18 hours and

180+ days are subject to the influence of the parents and the community. Unless the parents and community are involved, student behavior and motivation will be more influenced by what happens outside the school day. We explain how to involve parents and community and influence what happens outside the school with a character education program in chapter 5.

We have school culture and climate data on many schools and the data on levels of openness and trust are always the lowest. There is little agreement among faculty that they are open and trusting with each other. This creates a guarded environment where energy is being spent in a protective mode. Motivation that should go toward improving instruction is diverted toward making sure teachers stay out of trouble. Improving levels of openness and trust is a thread throughout the book, as is the concept of servant leadership. If administrators and teachers are perceived as servants as opposed to being perceived as self-serving individuals, an improvement in levels of openness and trust will result.

In *Creating a High-Performing School Culture*, the authors describe a comprehensive school-reform approach that addresses the six areas of a high-performing school culture and reduces resistance to school reform. Creating a "high-performing" school culture is an organizational approach to school reform that creates a distinctly different school culture and climate than can be found in existing schools. The authors detail a vision and mission for a comprehensive school reform that involves all stakeholders and leads to high performance.

The authors wrote an earlier version of the reform described in this book. There was a first and second edition but the first edition was too lengthy and somewhat eclectic. The second edition was lacking several components that did not enhance the reform. This is a revised version of the earlier books and the new version will consist of two books: Book #1 describes how to create and implement the reform and Book #2 describes how to enhance the reform. The title of the second book, under separate cover, is *"Enhancing a School's Culture and Climate.* Book #2 complements the reform efforts of Book #1. However, the reform described in Book #1 stands alone and does not require implementation of processes described in Book #2.

ORIGIN OF THE VISION AND MISSION

Many schools have a mission of developing a positive school culture designed to improve the quality of instruction, leading to high student test scores. However, it is often the case that the vision to achieve that mission has not been successfully communicated to all stakeholders. During the past 40 years, one of the authors, Dr. Clete Bulach, has held positions as a teacher, principal, superintendent, and college professor in a department of educational leadership. He had difficulty communicating a vision of how to create a culture that leads to high performance on the part of faculty and students.

Dr. Bulach was the external evaluator for character. In the fall of 2001, the West Virginia Legislature passed HB 2208 mandating the evaluation of the character education program of every school district in the state. Bulach was awarded the contract to evaluate each school district in the state during the 2002–2003 school years. Character and culture data were collected from 55 high schools, 55 middle schools, and 55 elementary schools. The data collected during these evaluations in Georgia and West Virginia helped to create the vision and mission for a high performance school.

He visited one school in each district and interviewed students, teachers, and administrators. During the interview, each of these stakeholder groups were asked what they liked and did not like about their school and what they liked and did not like about their school's character education program.

In Georgia too, culture/climate data and character data from faculty and students at six high schools, seven middle schools, and twelve elementary schools were collected. In reflecting on the data collected in these two states, a clear vision emerged on how to create a culture for a high-performing school.

This vision includes the concepts of servant leadership, organizational culture and climate, the use of authority and power, community building, and character education, and the use of a variety of strategies and diagnostic tools. The authors' extensive firsthand experience in dealing with programs in many schools in many states has provided them with expertise, tools, and insights to be able to present a comprehensive program that will promote school success.

WHAT IS A HIGH-PERFORMING SCHOOL?

A high-performing school is one that has implemented a plan to address the six reform areas mentioned earlier. It is one where student achievement is high and student and teacher absenteeism is low. Student behavior is such that teachers seldom have to control them or tell them what to do. A disciplinary reform process that works is in place. This creates a learning environment where there is (a) greater time on task, (b) improved achievement scores, (c) improved teacher morale, (d) lower teacher absenteeism, (e) a lower student dropout rate, (f) reduced bullying behavior, and (g) improved parental support.

Another distinct feature of a high-performing school is that the student peer group is a positive, rather than a negative, force. The end result is a school culture where faculty and students are more open, trusting, and caring about each other, and there is a cooperative attitude. The focus is on what can be done to help one another, and everyone is involved in the decision-making process. The end result is students who graduate as responsible and productive citizens.

The key concept that changes the existing school culture is to give control to students without giving up control. The greatest fear of a teacher or school administrator is to lose control of discipline. We will provide data at the classroom and school level that proves educators can give control to students without giving up control. Teachers who had to stop teaching a number of times found that they could teach almost without interruption.

Three elementary schools and one middle school have implemented one part of this reform. After one semester of implementation, student off-task behavior had decreased by 76%. This allowed teachers more time to teach and less interruption of the learning process. There was also a reduction in office referrals, allowing school administrators more time to focus on other aspects of the job instead of being consumed with discipline issues.

The culture of control in each classroom and the entire school can be changed. Students will control each other, not only in the classroom, but also in the bathrooms, hallways, lunchroom, etc. This is one of the four major changes that create a high-performing school culture. Another word could be used. It could be called a "citizenship" school, because in this school culture students help each other, dropouts are reduced, and bullying behavior is reduced.

WHO SHOULD READ THIS BOOK?

This book contains valuable information for school administrators, and members of boards of education. They must be involved for a comprehensive school reform to work. Teachers, however, can also implement many of the ideas, strategies, and processes in their classrooms, even though other teachers and the administration are not involved. Professors in colleges of education will also find this book of value for any course on "the principalship" and a useful supplementary text for any educational administrator leadership course.

Professors who oversee student teachers will also find this text useful because of its approach to discipline. Many student teachers experience difficulties handling student misbehavior. This approach of giving control without giving it up will help them be more successful. Anyone who is critical of the current education process will find this an interesting read with its novel approach to the creation of a school's culture and climate.

REFERENCES

Balfanz, R., Bridgeland, J. M., Gruce, M., & Fox, J. H. (2013). *Building a Grad Nation: Progress and Challenge in Ending the High School Dropout Epidemic.* Annual Update. ED542115.

Colombo, G., & Osher, D. (2015). *Advancing School Discipline Reform. Education Leaders Report*, Vol1 (2), National Assessment of State Boards of Education.

Duncan, A. (2015, February). *School Improvement Grants: Progress Report from America's Great City Schools Council of the Great City Schools.* Retrieved 6-10-2015, from (http://www.ed.gov/news/press-releases/secretary-duncan-issues-statement-council-great-city-schools-report-progress-under-school-improvement-grants).

Balu, R., Zhu, P., Doolittle, F., Schiller, E., Jenkins, J., & Gersten, R. (2015, November). *Evaluation of Response to Intervention Practices for Elementary School Reading.* National Center for Education Evaluation, and Regional Assistance.

Gray, P. (2009, November, 2nd). *Why Students Don't Like School? Well, Duhhh. Psychology Today.*

National Center on Education and the Economy. (2007). *Tough choices or tough times:* The report of the new commission on the skills of the American workforce. San Francisco: John Wiley & Sons.

Introduction

In chapters 1 through 5, the authors describe a school-reform process to improve school climate and culture. There are four distinct phases for creating the culture and climate of a high-performing school. Each phase can stand alone, but the phases build on one another. For example, **Phase IV** on the character education program could be implemented without the other phases. It is suggested, however, that **Phase I** be implemented first. This is a comprehensive school reform that is designed to improve a school's culture and climate. It is also designed to improve student test scores, prevent student dropouts, and reduce bullying behavior.

Many educational reforms in the past have focused on the improvement of test scores. While test scores do provide some measure of school improvement, to focus primarily on test scores misses important aspects of why school improvement is needed. Low test scores are a symptom, not the problem.

The end goal is to improve test scores and most reforms try to do this by implementing a new curriculum, as the Common Core or No Child Left Behind initiatives have done. The end goal is always test scores, when the focus should be on the six areas that tend to impact test scores. An analogy would be automobiles and miles per gallon (MPG) as opposed to students and test scores. In the auto industry they investigate and focus on what causes improved MPG. They focus on those things that improve MPG such as horsepower, wind resistance, tire pressure, acceleration, vehicular weight, turbos, fuel injection, etc.

In education, the focus is on test scores and not the areas that impact test scores. Our research shows that there are six major areas that are relevant. They are the following:

- **Discipline:** Teachers have to stop teaching to correct student misbehavior, resulting in the loss of about 30 days of instructional process a year.
- **School culture and climate** are poor and cause a lack of motivation on the part of students and teachers.
- The **basic needs** of teachers and students are not being met.
- The way **power is used to control** students causes resistance and a lack of motivation.
- **Parent and community involvement:** School initiatives fail because of the lack of involvement of parents and community.
- The **lack of openness and trust** in most faculties creates an environment where constituents spend a lot of energy in a protective instead of a productive mode.

A process that makes improvements in each of these areas will be described in the following chapters. These improvements will cause an improvement in test scores, a decrease in dropouts, and bullying behavior.

The four types of school cultures observed during on-site visits to school districts in West Virginia are described in chapter 1. There is the "laissez-faire" low-performing school, the "traditional" underperforming school, the "enlightened traditional" above-average performing school, and the high-performing school. A high-performing school is one where faculty and students have cultivated a feeling of community, where they work together in a cooperative environment to help each other grow and become more responsible citizens. Implementing the high-performing school culture is **Phase I** of this comprehensive school reform.

Phase II requires the involvement of all faculty in a four-step process for reshaping the culture of the school. The desired culture is one where servant leadership is in place. This facilitates a caring learning environment where students and faculty are open and trusting with each other. This is the focus of chapters 2 and 3.

Phase III is a continuation of the process for creating a high-performing school. This phase requires the appropriate use of power to motivate and control students and all constituents in the school environment. There are five freeing forms of power that tend to improve the culture and climate and four controlling forms of power that, if overused, cause a poor culture and climate. However, if they are not used when needed, a poor culture and climate will also result. The appropriate use and misuse of the freeing and controlling forms of power and their role in creating a high-performing school are the focus of chapter 4.

Phase IV describes a character education program that involves the students, faculty, staff, parents, and community. This character education program complements the preceding three phases and promotes the feeling of community created in the high-performing school. How to implement this character education program, which does not require a curriculum or additional time during the school day, is the subject of chapter 5.

The reform described here can also be implemented at the classroom level. It works best if it is implemented at the school level so all students and faculty have the same vision and mission. If that is not possible, individual teachers can achieve meaningful results at the classroom level.

Chapter 1

Four Types of School Culture (Phase I)

PHASE I (CHANGE THE EXISTING CULTURE OF CONTROL)

In this chapter, four distinct types of school cultures and the leadership style that created them are described. One of the four types of school cultures is the high performing one and implementing that type is what the rest of the book is about. In this first chapter, we describe how to implement Phase I of the high performing school culture. The four types of school cultures are:

- **The high-performing school culture** (2%–5%). This is a highly demanding school culture with high standards for conduct and academic performance. There is a caring and nurturing learning environment that is a part of the servant leadership concept embraced by both administrators and teachers.
- **The enlightened traditional school culture** (10%–15%). This is an above-average performing school that also has a demanding school culture, but the administration and teachers are not as responsive to the needs of others. The focus leans more to self-serving leadership rather than to servant leadership.
- **The traditional school culture** (60%–75%). This is an average to under-performing school. School officials are demanding, but the focus on control leads to a prison-like culture. This definitely does not meet the needs of students or faculty because self-serving leadership tends to focus on the administrators and faculty rather than on students and learning.
- **The laissez-faire school culture** (2%–5%). This is a low-performing school that is neither demanding nor responsive. Faculty and student performances are loosely monitored and accountability is very lax. The focus throughout the school tends to be focused on self or a "what's in it for me mentality."

These four types of school cultures were observed while making on-site visits and conducting interviews with faculty and students at 55 individual schools in West Virginia. Dr. Bulach served as the external evaluator for the four-year West Virginia character education grant (2002–2005). He conducted interviews and made on-site visits to each of the 55 school districts in the state. He logged 5,000 miles and spent five months visiting one school in each district. Two sets of students were interviewed. One comprised student leaders and the other comprised a randomly selected set of classroom students. The teachers at each school were interviewed using a "force-field analysis" technique (described in chapter 2).

All schools, because of the values and beliefs of the school community, had an established culture. As a result of this underlying culture, various rules and expectations were in place. A key component of any school's climate is the control culture. How faculty and students are controlled determines the type of school culture and climate. In addition to the control culture, the leadership style of the principal often plays a key role in shaping a school's culture. Keep in mind that a school can be a blend between two or more cultures. The leadership style we recommend is called servant leadership, and there will be more on this style later in the chapter and book.

In this chapter, we will also describe the role of control for implementing Phase I of the reform process for creating a high-performing school. Prior to implementing the "high-performing" school culture, school officials must identify the type of school culture that exists at their school. Describing the four types of school cultures assists with that process. We will present the least desirable school culture and end with the one we recommend for the comprehensive reform process.

THE LAISSEZ-FAIRE (LOW-PERFORMING SCHOOL)

A laissez-faire school is a low-performing school and it is characterized by a lack of control. There are not many schools with this type of culture, but they do exist. Based on our collective experience, we estimate that the number of schools with this type of culture is around 2%–5%. During school evaluations in West Virginia, several schools with this type of culture were observed. They had the following characteristics:

- The principal spends a lot of time in the office.
- The front office tends to be noisy.
- The secretary tends to be in charge of the front office.
- There may be a number of people waiting for the secretary to admit them to school.

- The principal does not have procedures in place to make sure all teachers are in their classrooms at the start of school.
- The procedures for discipline are not always followed.
- Teachers may be observed sitting at their desk grading papers instead of teaching.
- Students will be sitting in classrooms talking to each other instead of studying.
- Students will be found in hallways during class periods without passes.
- Teachers can be found in the teachers' lounge instead of in their classroom.
- Bus-loading procedures are not being followed.

In a laissez-faire school, the principal does not have procedures in place to control the faculty, and the teachers do not have procedures in place to control the students.

A variation of this type is a school where procedures are in place, but teachers do not follow them, and the principal does not follow through to make sure procedures are carried out. The leadership style tends to be nondirective, and the principal tends to ask people to do things, However, there tends to be little follow-through to make sure requests are acted on. Faculty and students tend to be self-serving, and there is an absence of servant leadership. Servant leadership will be described in detail in chapter 2.

In interviewing students and teachers of a school with this type of school culture, some of the negative comments were as follows:

- Some teachers punish the whole class when one student is the problem.
- Teachers and the principal have favorites. They will punish some kids and the same thing goes unpunished for the ones they like—particularly the dress code.
- The dress code and other rules are not enforced. Some teachers look the other way.
- The punishment does not always fit the crime.
- New students are not accepted.
- There is a lack of organization.
- People are judgmental.
- They don't care about us. All they care about is their paycheck.

THE TRADITIONAL (AVERAGE TO UNDERPERFORMING SCHOOL)

A second type of school culture is the traditional school, and it is characterized by a heavy emphasis on control. It is an underperforming school, and we estimate that approximately 60%–75% of the schools have this type of culture. The principal and the administrative team are very much in control. Teachers are submissive to the leadership team and are not involved in the decision-making process. There may be a leadership team, but in interviewing teachers on this topic, they responded that decisions made by the team tended to be what the principal wanted. They felt that the leadership team was a rubber stamp for the principal.

Every traditional school has a faculty handbook, and there are procedures established for everything that is supposed to happen at the school. Lesson plans are submitted on a daily basis, and everything is checked to make sure everyone is covering the required curriculum for that week. The same is true for students. Teachers are very much in control of what happens in each classroom with a heavy emphasis on discipline. In some districts, the tests are made at the central office. Teachers teach to cover material that will be on the test. The content that teachers are to teach is heavily controlled by the central office.

Students are not involved in what happens at the school. There is no student council or student leadership team. If one does exist, it has no decision-making power. It is a rubber stamp for the administration. The leadership style is directive, and position, reward, and coercion are the three forms of power most often used to control students and faculty. Coercion power in the form of punishment is the most frequently used form of power. There are six other forms of power in addition to these three. The nine forms of power, and their use and misuse, are described in chapter 4 (Phase III).

In one school when students were asked what they liked about their school, they had little to say. Several comments about what they liked were, "When school is out!" and "When I get off the bus!" When asked what they did not like, they were hesitant to talk. One student asked, "Will we get in trouble if we tell you things?" When they were assured that all comments were anonymous, and no one would know who said what, it was difficult to keep them quiet. Everyone wanted to talk. Their frustrated and angry comments were the following:

- Some teachers are nice but a lot of them are not nice.
- Some teachers cuss and call students names.
- Teachers have favorites. They will punish some kids, and the same thing goes unpunished for the ones they like.
- The teachers have double standards. They won't let us do things, but they do them. (Eating and drinking in their room was an example given.)
- The principal is mean.
- I do not like anything about it.
- The teachers put us down and ignore us.

- They don't care about us.
- The teachers do not help us when we need it.

In this type of school, faculty and the administration use grades and punishment to motivate the students. If students do not study, they receive an F. If they do not obey rules, they are punished. These are forms of extrinsic motivation and one of the major reasons why the schools are underperforming. Students tend to do what they have to do to stay out of trouble and get the grade they want. A teacher in one of these schools said, "If you give the students any freedom, they get out of control." The administration and teachers in this type of school have to constantly be on watch to make sure students do what they are supposed to do.

The majority of schools in the United States fall into this category. The heavy emphasis on control creates a culture and climate similar to that of a prison. Silva and Mackin (2002) wrote: "Next to prisons, high schools are the least democratic institutions in our American society. They are cursed by a tradition of hypocrisy—teaching and espousing democratic doctrine within the classroom, but doing it in a highly controlled authoritarian manner that makes the actual practice of democratic principles largely nonexistent anywhere in the school" (p. 1).

Most students do not like this type of school, as Peter Gray (2009) notes in his book *Why Students Don't Like School*. He wrote that you can ask any schoolchild what they don't like about school and they will tell you that school is a prison. He says that students may be too polite to say it, but if you decipher what they are saying the translation generally is that school is a prison.

This opinion is supported by Kohn (2006, 2004), who stated that there is an overreliance on punishment as a way of disciplining students who do not follow rules. He wrote that school officials' response to discipline with ever-harsher measures is counterproductive. The next type of school culture attempts to address this overreliance on punishment.

A recent publication by Colombi and Osher (2015) supports the above belief that traditional forms of punishment do not work. They stated that administrator and teacher efforts to control student misbehavior often backfire. This kind of reactive and punitive response diverts valuable time from the instructional practice and contributes to teacher burnout.

Lewis (2015) agrees with the opinions of those who state that discipline practices of traditional school cultures do not work. She wrote that negative consequences, punishment, and timeouts just make bad behavior worse. She believes that traditional discipline uses consequences to control students and the more you try to control them, the more they dig their heels in, and nobody is going to win. She believes you have to give students control without giving it up. Asking them questions, listening to them, and giving them space is one way to do that. There has to be a shift from controlling behavior to meeting a child's needs and solving problems.

THE ENLIGHTENED TRADITIONAL (ABOVE-AVERAGE PERFORMING SCHOOL)

A third type of school culture is an enlightened traditional school, and it is an above-average performing school. We estimate that approximately 10%–15% of schools have some variation of this type of culture. The principal and administrative teams are also very much in control; however, they have created incentives or reinforcers for faculty and students to control themselves. Instead of relying on position and coercion to control faculty and students, the administration has an established system of rewards to encourage faculty and students to control themselves.

This is an attempt to shift control from the leaders to subordinates and from teachers to students. For example, if teachers and students control their behavior and do what they are supposed to do, there is a reward. Some examples of incentives or rewards are as follows:

- **Teacher of the year**: Teachers are recognized at a board meeting and given a parking spot close to the school entrance as a way to encourage them to go the extra mile.
- **Leadership team**: Teachers are chosen by the principal to provide advice and assist with the communication process when needed.
- **Student of the month**: Each teacher has a student of the month, or sometimes only one is chosen for the entire school as a way to recognize attendance, character behavior, citizenship, and so forth. Other variations can be students who are recognized at the end of a grading period, the end of the semester, or the end of the year.
- **Points system**: Students who do what they are supposed to do regarding homework, attendance, and behavior earn points. These points can be cashed in at the student store for pencils, paper, or other school-related items or for treats in the cafeteria.
- **Redirects, reminders, or violations**: Students who do not do what they are supposed to do are given a redirect. The redirect can be for any rule infraction or failure to exhibit a behavior related to a character trait. If a student receives three redirects in one day, a punishment is incurred. At the end of a grading period, all students who have incurred no punishments in the form of office referrals or less than three redirects are rewarded with a field trip or something else that the students have requested. One school

has a "movie madness" afternoon where students select a movie they want to watch, and business partners provide food and drinks.
- **Caught doing good**: A certificate is given to students who do good deeds. This can be related to the character word for the month or any other deed that a teacher deems worthy of recognition. Some schools provide treats or rewards for each certificate and recognize students during morning announcements.

In the enlightened traditional school, both punishment and reward are used to motivate and/or control students. The motivation is still extrinsic, but there is an improvement in student behavior. According to the research of Marzano, Marzano, and Pickering (2003), there is a 24% increase in student misbehavior where there are no consequences, a 28% decrease where there are consequences, a 31% decrease if there are rewards for positive behavior, and a 33% decrease if both punishment and rewards are used.

Marzano and colleagues (2003) stated, "The guiding principle for disciplinary interventions is that they should include a healthy balance between negative consequences for inappropriate behavior and positive consequences for appropriate behavior" (p. 40). Kohn (2006), however, stated that this type of discipline does not help students to grow to be responsible students. He believes that students should control their behavior because it is the right thing to do and not because of a reward.

The controversy over the use of rewards has been ongoing. According to Sergiovanni, Starratt, and Cho (2013), the use of rewards is not a good practice because student behavior is motivated for external reasons. The desired behavior occurs because of the reward and not because it is the right thing to do. They believe that students should not be rewarded (external motivation) for a good action as it extinguishes the internal motivation to do the right thing. Intermittent reward, however, according to these theorists does not extinguish internal motivation.

Several schools were observed using intermittent rewards for students "caught doing good." They received a "caught doing good" certificate and personal recognition. The certificate was put in a box, and at the end of the week, several names were drawn from the box. Those students received a prize from the school's business partners. One school drew two names and their business partner, a bank, gave each student a $50 savings bond.

Another variation of "caught doing good" is the ability of students to trade in a number of "caught doing good" certificates to remove a redirect or reminder. In some schools, students who have more than three redirects, reminders, or violations are excluded from the end-of-grading-period reward. The intent here was to present students with the opportunity to get back into the good graces of school officials. Supposedly, once a student knows they are excluded from the end-of-grading-period reward, there is no incentive for them to behave other than traditional discipline procedures.

The ability to trade "caught doing good" certificates for rule infractions is an incentive for the so-called "bad actors" to continue trying to improve their behavior. In schools that use point systems instead of certificates, students can use points to buy back a violation or redirect. This practice encourages desirable behavior by rewarding it while continuing to punish undesirable behavior.

Many enlightened traditional schools do not have a plan in place to motivate students who have lost the chance to take part in the end-of-report-period reward. This is a mistake as there is no motivation for these students to behave once they have lost the opportunity to take part in the reward. A system should be put in place so they can earn back the right to take part.

One of the comments frequently heard from students during interviews with them was that the character education program had no effect on the bad actors. These bad actors are typically 5%–7% of the students, and they are the students who make it difficult for teachers to teach and other students to learn. A plan has to be developed to encourage these students to control their disruptive behavior.

An interesting variation of "caught doing good" was observed at a middle school, and it involved the use of a character bulletin board. Teachers who saw a student doing something representative of the character trait being taught would put a post-it note with the student's name on the bulletin board. The note was put there after the students went home. In the morning, before classes started, students looked at the bulletin board to see if their name was there. If it was, they took it to the teacher who put it there, and then three things happened.

- The teacher verbally reinforced the student's positive behavior.
- The student was given a treat.
- The post-it note was put in a jar in the office.

A post-it was periodically drawn from the jar, and that student and the teacher were given a prize. The teacher's reward was a free period while the principal taught the class. The students' treat or prize can be as small as a pencil or an ice cream at lunch or a McDonald's meal or something larger from another business partner.

The intriguing part was the interest and excitement created by not rewarding the behavior when it happened. Instead students had to check the bulletin board each morning to see who had been caught being good. When students at this school were interviewed, they said they really liked the character bulletin board and the excitement it generated when they took their name off the board and went to the teacher, cook, or other person who put their name there to find out what they had done. Teachers also liked having the principal take their class for a period. This was observed in an elementary school. We are not sure if it would work in a high or middle school.

Marzano and colleagues (2003) stated that behavior limits need to be established and that a record-keeping system must be in place. In some schools it means having a pencil, finishing homework, having textbooks, raising hands, not getting out of seats unless permitted, walking on the right side of the hall, following the dress code, and so forth. Students with too many violations lose their freedom at lunch. Too many violations can be as few as one to as many as five. Instead of going to lunch and perhaps recess with the other students, misbehaving students get their lunch and report to a separate room where they are counseled on what they have to do to earn back the right to eat lunch with the other students.

In an enlightened traditional school, a system is in place to encourage students and others to control their own behavior. The burden of controlling what people are supposed to do is shared with everyone in the school. Students and faculty are given the freedom to control their own behavior, and incentives are in place to encourage desirable behavior. If students and faculty do not control their own behavior and undesirable behavior is the result, then someone controls them and does something to extinguish the undesirable behavior.

This is in contrast to the traditional school where students and faculty have little freedom. Students are controlled by teachers, and teachers are controlled by the administration. They must do what they are supposed to or they will receive admonishment or punishment. The leadership style in a traditional school tends to be authoritarian and in an enlightened traditional school tends to be collaborative. The forms of power used in a traditional school tend to be position, reward, and coercion power.

The forms of power used in an enlightened traditional school are information, personality, ego, and moral power. Position and coercion power are used when the preceding forms of power do not work. Servant leadership can take place in this type of school, but the focus on getting a reward tends to be self-serving. The forms of power and servant leadership will be discussed in detail in chapter 4.

THE HIGH-PERFORMING SCHOOL

A fourth type of school culture is the high-performing school. We estimate that there are approximately 2%–5% with this type of culture. We know one such school in West Virginia and several in Indiana. The school in West Virginia was the impetus for this chapter and the book. The high-performing school has many of the same features as the enlightened traditional school, but it has added an additional reward for desirable behavior.

While the enlightened traditional school relies on individuals to control their own behavior, the high-performing school creates an incentive or reward for the peer group to help control other students. For example, if there are no redirects, reminders, or violations or if they are less than a prescribed number, the peer group gets a reward. This can take many forms. The peer group can be a class of students, a team, an advisory group, a homeroom, a grade level, or the entire school. The larger the peer group, the more students are involved in controlling the other students.

Ideally, the entire school should be involved, but it has been successful in a single classroom as well. This system requires setting a benchmark for the students to try to reach or stay under. For example, if office referrals for the entire school for a week totaled 100, the benchmark can be set at 50. If the number of office referrals for the next week were under that benchmark, all the students are given a reward. The reward can be a recess, board games, or some other compensation that is a motivator.

In a high-performing school all students receive the reward, whereas in an enlightened traditional school only those students who have behaved responsibly get the reward. In a high-performing school peer pressure on those students who are disruptive does occur. There is also an additional incentive for disruptive students to do what they are supposed to do because they will also enjoy the reward, whereas in the enlightened traditional setting, they are excluded.

Office referrals can be used to establish benchmarks, but a better system uses redirects, reminders, or pink slips. There is a lot of student behavior that does not warrant punishment, but it does interfere with creating a caring learning environment. Responsible student behavior must be encouraged. The redirects, reminders, or pink slips are one way to encourage responsible student behavior without punishing students every time they forget to do what they are supposed to do.

Only one high-performing school was observed during the on-site visits and interviews in West Virginia. School officials at this middle school set a benchmark and reward for each day, as well as an end-of-report-period reward for students with fewer than three redirects during the period. Their benchmark was 25 or fewer redirects for a day. If that benchmark was met, the reward was 10 extra minutes of locker time the next day. This particular school had approximately 350 students, and they met their benchmark on an average of four times per week. On the day of the visit, they had fewer than ten redirects, and the reward was an extra ten minutes of free time before dismissal.

When asked to describe a redirect, the principal stated that any time a teacher had to reprimand a student for not raising their hand, running, wearing a cap, talking, and so forth, it was considered a redirect. When asked how state guidelines for time requirements were addressed, the principal stated that students have more "time on task" at his school because teachers had fewer interruptions of the instructional process. He stated that when they started this system ten years ago, the benchmark was 100 redirects per day and each year the benchmark has been lowered. Currently the benchmark is 25 per day.

While there was only one high-performing school, a number of teachers were seen in other schools who used some variation of the high-performing school system at the classroom level. Some teachers used movies and pop-corn, but this was not a strong motivator because students had often already seen the movie. Some used field trips, which tend to be strong motivators.

The strongest motivator is free time. Students want time to interact with their friends. If the reward is a weekly event, a strong motivator is extra time on Friday to go to the gym or playground and hang out or play games. If the reward for reducing the number redirects is a daily event, five minutes of extra time at recess is a very strong motivator. At the elementary level, the ability to delay gratification is difficult for students. Extra recess is a very strong motivator because they know at the end of the day whether they have met their target. Choosing a reward that will motivate the peer group to become active in controlling each other is extremely important.

An elementary school that was visited had a banner displayed outside the classroom with the fewest redirects for the month. A classroom was visited where a teacher had two jars of marbles. She told her students if they had a good day, she would take a handful of marbles from jar 1 and put it into jar 2. When the jar 1 was empty and jar 2 full, the entire class could go to McDonald's for ice cream. She had some other rules regarding the marbles:

- If they had a bad day, she would remove a handful of marbles from jar 2 and place them back in jar 1 or vice versa if they had a good day.
- If a student did something good, she might take a marble from jar 1 and place it in jar 2.
- If a student did something bad, she might take a marble out of jar 2 and place it back in jar 1.

Through use of the marbles and the jars, this teacher created a high-performing classroom and an incentive for the students to help each other to behave responsibly. Another variation of this classroom control/incentive technique involved the use of a paper chain. The teacher added a link to the chain when the class did what they were supposed to do. When the chain reached a certain length, the entire class got a reward. When there were only a few marbles left in jar 1 or only a few more links to add to the chain, student behavior was wonderful. They worked together because they knew the reward was soon to come.

One interesting observation about the high-performing school or classroom is that it teaches a very important character trait—citizenship. It creates a community within a classroom, grade level, team, or school where students are encouraged to be responsible citizens. They follow rules, obey authority, help each other, intervene when something wrong is about to happen or is happening, and so forth. They learn to recognize undesirable behavior and model-desirable behavior.

This type of school creates an environment where students learn to become responsible citizens. The leadership style, as in an enlightened traditional school, tends to be collaborative. The interesting transformation, however, is that control has been shifted to students. They are being asked to help control each other whereas in the past, it was the teachers and administrators' responsibility to control students.

This shift in control changes the peer group from a negative force to a positive force. Berger (2003) writes:

> I was raised with the message that peer pressure was something terrible, something to avoid, or something negative. Peer pressure meant kids trying to talk you into smoking cigarettes or taking drugs. I realized after ten years of teaching that positive peer pressure was the primary reason my classroom was a safe, supportive environment for student learning. Peer pressure wasn't something to be afraid of or to be avoided, but rather to be cultivated in a positive direction. (p. 36)

In most classrooms, peer pressure is still a negative force. Changing the existing control culture gives control to the peer group and makes it a positive force.

THE ROLE OF CONTROL IN A HIGH-PERFORMING SCHOOL

A culture has been created in most schools where control issues are a major factor. Boards control superintendents, who control central office, who control principals, who control teachers, who control students. It is all about control. Most school officials believe they have to have control and in fact **they do have to control**. Losing control is one of the greatest fears of any educator, whether teacher, administrator, or board member. Control has to be there! Learning cannot occur in a school where there is not a highly controlled environment.

While that is true, think for a minute about how it feels when you have lost control or are not in control versus how you feel when you are in control. It is as different as night and day. In a school environment, everyone is in a highly controlled environment. While everyone wants to be in an environment where things are under control, very few people like to be controlled.

A successful marriage or relationship has both elements: It should be a controlled setting that gives control. If a marriage or relationship is to be successful, someone has to be in control of what happens. However, if the other person or people in the relationship feel like they are being controlled, they will not be happy. It is a universal principle that human beings like to have some feeling of control.

That is not the case for students in most schools across the country. Students must follow the rules and study what is on their schedule. Students are controlled and have little control over what happens. As stated earlier most school cultures are similar to that of a prison. That is one of the major reasons why many students are unmotivated and dropout. The lack of motivation is also one of the major causes of low test scores.

Teachers are also in a highly controlled environment and must do what the administration tells them to do. Administrators must carry out the mandates of their states' Department of Education. No one, teacher, student, or principal, likes to be in a situation where they feel controlled. Yet that is what is happening in school after school across the United States. This causes a number of problems resulting in low test scores, student absenteeism, poor school culture and climate, high dropout rates, and high teacher absenteeism on Mondays and Fridays.

How does this relate to the culture of control that exists in schools? When student misbehavior occurs, students do nothing because they expect the administration or teachers to control the situation. It is not okay for students to intervene because they are in a highly controlled environment. Students are controlled and are not expected to exert control on other students. If a student were to exert control on another student, they would be asked: "Who do you think you are?" They might be called the teacher's pet or something else. A culture has been created where students are not encouraged to control other students.

Are there schools that are exceptions to this generalization? One exception would be JROTC units, in which students are expected to control underclassmen. Perhaps that is why they are so successful. Montessori schools could be another exception.

One interesting observation about the high-performing school or classroom is that students are given control, but control has not been given up. It also teaches a very important character trait—citizenship. It creates a community within a classroom, grade level, team, or school where students are encouraged to control each other and be responsible citizens. They follow rules, obey authority, help each other, and intervene when something wrong is about to happen or is happening.

They learn to recognize undesirable behavior and model-desirable behavior. They realize that it is their responsibility to intervene when their peers' behavior is inappropriate. In the three other types of school cultures, controlling students' behavior is the responsibility of the faculty and the administration.

The existing culture of control in most schools creates another problem. That problem is bullying behavior. When bullying behavior occurs, the other students become bystanders as they watch it take place. According to Beane and Bulach (2009) and Beane (2009), 53% of students reported that they stand and watch and do nothing. In fact, they tend to support the bully instead of trying to stop the bully.

This happens because it is not their responsibility to take control of the situation. That is the responsibility of the faculty and the administration. So they gather around and watch until someone intervenes and stops the behavior. In the high-performing school culture, students realize that they are supposed to take control of the situation and stop that kind of behavior. In this type of control culture, the peer group becomes a positive force.

DOES THE HIGH-PERFORMING CONCEPT REALLY WORK?

While the above statements are based on observations and opinion, are there data that support the belief that they really work? How difficult is it to implement the high-performing concept in a classroom or school? To answer these questions, an experiment was designed where 30 graduate students in educational leadership classes agreed to try it with their own students. One limitation was that it was implemented at **the classroom level** and not at the **school level**. The research design was as follows:

Procedure

- Each graduate student was a teacher in a public school setting.
- Each graduate student counted for five weeks the number of redirects for his or her students. At the end of the five-week period, they calculated the average number of redirects per day and/or week.
- Students were not told that they were part of an experiment.
- At the end of five weeks, the students were told of the average number of redirects and were asked to help the teacher lower the average number. If they were successful, the entire class would receive a reward.
- Students were asked to select a reward that would be a good motivator.

Results

The number of redirects for students in each graduate student's classroom was reduced by more than 50%. A description of how the high-performing classroom concept worked in selected classrooms across the K-12 spectrum is as follows:

- In a kindergarten class, there was an average of 51 redirects per day for five weeks pre-experiment. During the five weeks post-experiment, there was an average of 13 redirects per day. To make the class aware of their progress regarding the number of redirects, cubes were added to a jar for good behavior, and cubes were removed for redirects. Students were rewarded when the jar was full.
- In a third-grade class, there was an average of 20 redirects per week pre-experiment and an average of less than 10 redirects per week post-experiment.
- At a middle school, in four classes, there was an average of 31 redirects per class per day and 585 per week pre-experiment compared to 13 redirects per day per class and 244 per week post-experiment.
- In a middle school emotional disorder class, there was average of 50 to 83 redirects per week pre-experiment compared to an average of 12 to 28 per week post-experiment. In commenting about what happened, the teacher wrote, "They were strongly motivated not to let each other down. I could not believe the improvement in their behavior. One week there was a sub, and they only had 28 violations. I could not believe they were able to keep it together."
- In a middle-school physical education class, the redirects ranged from an average of 32 to 63 per week during the five weeks pre-experiment compared to 10 to 25 per week post-experiment.
- In a 10th-grade English class, the average number of redirects was 35 per week and 7 per day pre-experiment and less than 1 per day post-experiment.
- A science teacher reported an average number of redirects of 60 per week for chemistry and 55 per week in biology pre-experiment and 25 per week in chemistry and 15 per week in biology post-experiment. This teacher commented that the students improved each week, and by the last week of the experiment, the chemistry class had only 10 redirects per week and the biology class only 8. In summarizing the results of the experiment, the teacher wrote, "My students have really taken charge of their behavior. I have seen outstanding results, and many teachers have commented on the change in my class."

In each of the above instances the students received a reward when the goal was reached. The selection of the reward is crucial. It has to be something they really want. Let them choose it, but give them some examples, such as free time on Friday, a pizza party, get rid of a low grade, being able to chew gum, recess, an open-book test, homework passes, and so forth.

If the high-performing concept is implemented at the classroom level, a weekly reward works best. If it is implemented at the school level, a daily or a weekly reward can be used. The best motivator is 10 extra minutes of locker time in the morning or 10 extra minutes prior to getting on the bus at the end of the day. Keep in mind that students can earn redirects during this extra 10 minutes.

Why does this work so well? According to Stetson, Hurley, and Miller (2003), "Humans have two strong and conflicting desires: To become more autonomous, and to be connected to other humans" (p. 129). In a high-performing school, students have some feeling of control and ownership. Whether they get the reward is strictly up to them and the peer group.

The environment created by the high-performing school allows students to satisfy the autonomy and connection, but in this setting, they are not conflicting. They have a feeling of control (**autonomy**) because they understand what is expected of them, and they willingly choose to do the right thing. Doing the right thing is called moral power (discussed in chapter 4). The motivation is intrinsic, they are independent, they are empowered, and they are in control. At the same time, because the reward can only be achieved through a cooperative effort of the peer group, they have a **connection** with other students.

There is perhaps another reason why the high-performing school or classroom works so well. Joftus (2002), based on the research of others, stated that 40% of high-school youth and 50% of middle school youth feel disengaged. Further, he stated that rates are even higher in urban and minority schools. This leads to students simply giving up because they are bored, frustrated, and feel under appreciated. They feel that no one cares. In support of this opinion, Bulach, Fullbright, and Williams (2003) surveyed students on bullying behavior and found that 50% of them reported that "people do not care about each other at our school." In a high-performing school or classroom, the peer group cares about the behavior of other students.

Four schools in Indiana have implemented Phase I of this book, where the control culture was shifted to students **at the school level**. Three elementary schools and one middle school implemented Phase I and the results were amazing. The number of teachers in the four schools was 114 and the number of students was 2,175. The following procedures were used: Sometime during the first month of the school year and prior to implementing any part of the reform, each teacher in all four schools counted the number of times they had to correct or redirect student behavior for a week. Redirects were counted in the classroom, hallways, lunchroom, and other parts of the school. The procedures used are the following:

- The teachers used clickers to count redirects for a week.
- After that week, the students were asked to help control each other's behavior; that is, control was shifted to students. Teachers did not give up control, but asked students to help control each other.
- Students were told that they would get extra recess time (elementary schools) or locker time (middle school) if they could reduce the number of times teachers had to control them or redirect student behavior.

The schools had an average of 2,402 redirects a day during the pre-implementation week for all four schools. One teacher (a special education teacher) had an average of 229 redirects a day, while others had only 10–50 a day. A great deal of time and effort was being exerted to control students, and that was time taken away from teaching. The teacher with 229 redirects a day was averaging almost one redirect each minute. After 11 weeks of implementing the process, the number of redirects each day was down from 2,402 (pre-implementation) to 595 (post-implementation).

The existing culture, in which the teachers were expected to control student behavior, was changed. The new culture was one in which the students were being asked to control each other's behavior. It was now okay for students to control each other whereas in the past it was not legitimate for students to do that. For example, if students were misbehaving, one of the other students was expected to intervene and stop it. In most schools, students are not expected to intervene because that is the responsibility of the teachers and administrators.

What happened (post-experiment) was astounding! The students loved the new culture and went about controlling their own behavior and that of the other students with gusto. Every teacher reported a 50% or greater reduction in redirects. The teacher with 229 redirects **a day** (pre-experiment) averaged 35 a day after 11 weeks (85% reduction). One teacher, who averaged five redirects a day (pre-experiment), had zero (100% reduction) redirects a day (post-experiment).

All off-task behaviors were reduced, resulting in greater time on task. The teachers at these four schools in September 2009 (pre-implementation) stopped teaching to redirect students 2,402 times a day. After 11 weeks of implementation of Phase I of the reform process, that dropped to 595 or a decrease of 76%.

Once the new control culture becomes ingrained and students become more accustomed to controlling each other's behavior, there will be even fewer redirects. Implementing this process of shifting control to students at the school level creates a fundamental change in a school's culture and climate. Several principals reported that there were fewer office referrals as well.

The middle school that implemented the reform also collected pre-implementation data on school culture and climate and the character behavior of the students. We wanted to determine if the reform positively affected these two variables. A t-test ($p < 0.05$) for independent groups was the statistical analysis used to compare the pre-data from the spring of 2009 (pre-implementation) with the data from the spring of 2010 (post-implementation).

The overall mean on the school's culture and climate scores had improved significantly after one year of implementing the reform. The culture variable with the largest improvement was "group cooperation." The climate variables with the largest improvements were "discipline" and "sense of mission." A comparison of the character behavior scores pre- to post- did show an improvement but it was not statistically significant.

The data from the middle school support the earlier findings of Bulach and Malone (1994), who also found a significant relationship between school climate and the implementation of a reform. Bulach (2006) in reporting on the character grant data in West Virginia found a significant relationship of $r = +0.475$, ($p < 0.01$) between culture/climate scores and character scores. A correlation of $r = +0.57$ ($p < 0.05$) was also found between the character data and student achievement. These correlations were not only significant but also represent a large effect size. This means the correlations were both statistically significant and important.

In other research on these variables, Bulach (2006) looked at relationships between character scores and the individual culture and climate variables. The climate variable with the highest correlation with character scores ($r = +0.577$, $p < 0.01$) was parent involvement. Teacher expectations ($r = +0.536$, $p < 0.01$) followed by the way teachers teach ($r = +0.532$, $p < 0.01$) were the next highest correlations.

The climate variable with the strongest relationship to all other culture and climate variables is the leadership of the principal. The leadership of the principal, with a correlation of $r = 0.476$ ($p < 0.05$), also has a significant positive relationship with the character behavior of students. A significant relationship was also found between character behavior and the way discipline is administered ($r = +0.490$, $p < 0.01$).

Regarding comparisons of school culture and climate with student achievement, Bulach (2006) reported that they are positively related, with correlations ranging from a low of $r = +0.43$ to a high of $r = +0.57$. In earlier research, Bulach and Malone (1995) found a positive correlation of $r = +0.54$ with school climate and achievement. Based on the statistical data from previous research by Bulach, we can conclude that the variables of school culture, climate, character behavior of students, and student achievement are positively related. We also conclude that this school reform will improve school culture and climate, with an eventual improvement expected in student achievement and students' character behavior.

The title of this book indicates that improving school culture and climate will reduce the dropout rate and bullying behavior. We do not have data to verify that, but there is some recent research on this by Pearson (2015). The purpose of his research was to investigate the relationship between school culture in high schools and graduation and dropout rates. Thirty-three high schools in Mississippi were involved in the study. The results were that high schools that had a positive school culture had a lower dropout rate and a higher graduation rate. We believe that the changes in the control culture we advocate in this reform will also improve the overall school culture and climate.

A few questions that may come to mind as you read this are the following: Does this change in the school culture related to control last? Why does it work? Do you have to teach students how to control each other? Should you allow students to control each other? What if students can't control each other? It is our opinion that this change in the culture of control will last indefinitely. Keep in mind that the idea for coming up with this change in the culture of control was the result of a middle school visitation in West Virginia.

They had implemented a change in the control culture and were in their tenth year with the process. With a school population of 345 students, there were many days where there were fewer than 25 redirects each day. Based on their experience, we can say that once the process is implemented, the change in the control culture will continue to be successful.

As for why it works, the answer is very simple: In most schools, the only people controlling behavior are the faculty. In this changed control culture, you have the faculty and all the students who are watching for behavior that needs redirecting. In the average classroom, instead of one pair of eyes (the teacher's), you have 25 pairs of eyes (the students') plus the teacher, and that is why it is so effective in reducing off-task behavior.

The next question is, "Do students have to be taught how to control each other?" The answer is a definite "No!" One needs only to think of "peer pressure" to understand that students are very capable of controlling each other when it is okay to control and they want to do so. Peer pressure is a strong controlling force in any peer group. Within any school there are many different peer groups that exert control on their members. Changing the existing control culture creates a peer group for the whole school. All students are encouraged to help control each other and not just within their peer group.

Should you allow students to control each other? Isn't that what life is all about? Everyone is in control of something. We need to teach students how to control their life and those with whom they are involved. No one wants to be out of control and everyone wants to have some control. Allowing and encouraging students to control each other's behavior is what good citizens do. In the school reform culture being described in this chapter, students will not wait on faculty. They will realize that it is each student's responsibility to step up to the plate.

There are students who will not allow other students to control their behavior. Some students are so antisocial that they continue to be disruptive no matter what their peers say or do to them. If that happens, teachers should not count redirects for that student and should not encourage the peer group to control that student.

A novel approach by one teacher in Las Vegas, Nevada, who used the redirects to control students, was to give all students a 3 x 5 card, except the one student who was causing problems. They were asked to write a "y" or an "n" on the card if they wanted the student to be sent to the office for discipline. If they voted "yes" to send the student to the office there was no redirect. If they voted "no" a redirect was counted. Using this process, it was the students and not the teacher who sent the disruptive student for discipline.

Earlier, it was mentioned that this reform process should also reduce teacher absenteeism. Teacher absenteeism on Mondays and Fridays is much higher than the other days of the week. On some Mondays and Fridays there are so many teachers absent that it is difficult to find substitutes because all the substitute teachers have already been hired.

Stress is the reason why teachers have such a high rate of absenteeism in general and why absenteeism is higher on Mondays and Fridays. The more stress teachers experience the higher the absenteeism rate. What causes stress? There are many factors: Demands from the administration, declining test scores, disagreements with other faculty members, etc. However, one of the leading causes of stress is the need to control the students. Dearborn (2015) stated that the average teacher is tired of dealing with negative student behavior because "managing student behaviors eventually sucks the energy from most teachers, no matter how talented or experienced" (p. 1).

It is not uncommon for a teacher to have to correct students 150 times a day or, as in the case above, 229 times. That means that a teacher has to stop teaching and correct a student every 2–3 minutes. Having to stop teaching, correct a student, and restart teaching causes a lot of stress. By the time Friday rolls around, some teachers have had all they can take, so they are absent. Come Monday, some teachers don't want to go back to work because they are mentally just not able, so they stay home another day.

This constant interruption of the learning process, if it could be reduced, would add at least 30 days of instruction to the calendar year. For example, most teachers have to stop teaching, on an average, about five times each class period. Assume that two minutes are lost each time before the learning process restarts. That would be 10 minutes in each class period or 60 minutes for six classes a day.

Most schools have 180 days in a calendar year which would result in 180 hours a year lost to the instructional process or 30 days (180 hours divided by 6 hours = 30). Eliminating this loss would reduce teacher stress, improve test scores, reduce the dropout rate, and improve school culture and climate.

The data at the classroom and school level prove that educators can give control to students without giving up control. Teachers who had to stop teaching a number of times found that they could teach almost without interruption. The culture of control in each classroom and the entire school can be changed. Students will control each other, not only in the classroom, but also in the bathrooms, hallways, lunchroom, etc. Keep in mind that this is only Phase I for creating a high-performing school.

Another word for this kind of school is a "Citizenship" school, because in this kind of school, students help each other. If a student does not have a pencil, a book, their homework, etc., they help each other. It is human nature that people like to help each other. Change the existing control culture, and students will have many opportunities to practice good citizenship. A good citizen will not tolerate bullying behavior. They will not continue to be bystanders waiting for an adult to intervene.

How big a problem is bullying behavior? In 2009, the Departments of Education and Health and Human Services joined forces with four other departments to create a federal task force on bullying. In August 2010, the task force staged the first-ever National Bullying Summit, bringing together 150 top state, local, civic, and corporate leaders to begin mapping out a national plan to end bullying. The task force also launched a new website, www.bullyinginfo.org, which brings all the federal resources on bullying together in one place for the first time ever. A person who is being bullied or harassed can go to this site to find resources for help.

Additionally, the following was written after the 2011 White House Conference on Bullying Prevention:

> Every day, thousands of children, teens, and young adults around the country are bullied. Estimates are that nearly one-third of all school-aged children are bullied each year—upwards of 13 million students. Students involved in bullying are more likely to have challenges in school, to abuse drugs and alcohol, and to have health and mental health issues. If we fail to address bullying we put ourselves at a disadvantage for increasing academic achievement and making sure all of our students are college and career ready.

It is very clear from the above messages that bullying behavior is a problem in our society and schools. We believe this school reform will positively affect bullying behavior because good citizens step to the plate to stop bullying and do not continue to be bystanders.

A good citizen does not rely on others, such as police, fire department, or school officials to deal with a problem. They know that it is their responsibility to intervene and if they can't deal with the problem they call on a higher authority. In most schools today, they stand by and watch to see what the higher authority will do. I (Bulach) know this is what happens. While interviewing students in every school district in West Virginia, there was often a student who "acted out." The other students did nothing to this student who was "acting out." They wanted to see how I was going to deal with the misbehavior. In the high-performing school described in this chapter, the students would have handled it.

One area not addressed so far is how the school culture and climate described address the basic needs of all humans. What are their basic needs? If a person's needs are not being met what happens to motivation? According to Maslow's hierarchy, there are five needs that determine motivation: physiological, security, social, self-esteem, and self-actualization. According to Maslow (1943), learning or self-actualization will not occur if these needs are not being met.

While Maslow's hierarchy is well known, there is little research data that support the point that these are basic needs. What have others written about basic needs or why people behave the way they do? Should a school environment or culture address the basic needs of students and faculty? If needs are not being met, how does that affect motivation? We believe that it is very important that the needs of students and teachers should be met. If needs are not met, learning will be adversely affected. What are these needs?

Philosophers have been writing for centuries about these needs and why people behave the way they do. They write that people behave the way they do because they want to be **alive**. They write that people want to be **happy**. So far no surprises! Of course people want to be alive and happy. The next need that occurs in these early writings by philosophers of the late nineteenth and early twentieth centuries is the need for power or **control**. Nietzsche (1910) wrote that life and happiness are important, but the need to have power and control are more important. We agree that having some control of your life is very important. The feeling when control has been lost is awful versus the feeling of having control. Being in control is a great feeling.

Three basic needs have been described so far: life, happiness, and control. There are two other basic needs that need to be met if a learning environment for a high-performing school is to be created. Students need to have a purpose in their life and they need to know that they are cared for. Having some control in life means nothing if there is no purpose. Dr. Mehmet Oz in his TV show, Rick Warren in his book about a purpose-driven life, and the Dalai Lama on a 2012 TV show with Piers Morgan all stated that life without a purpose is no life.

Approximately 50% of all students go to school without a purpose. They go because that is the law. Students who go to school without a purpose misbehave, lack motivation, and score poorly in tests. Giving students a reward for improving student behavior gives them a purpose. Giving students a grade for studying is also a purpose, but many students do not care about grades, so there is no purpose and no motivation.

The last of the five basic needs necessary for a high-performing school culture is caring. Students and faculty need to know/feel that others care about them. The easiest way to show someone that you care is to "listen" to them. When you give someone your attention and listen to them you are showing them that you care. The way you behave in the presence of others and your nonverbal behavior also project caring. Caring behaviors can be seen and they are also felt. Students who correct misbehavior and help others are demonstrating caring behaviors.

In summary, the five basic needs are life, caring, control, purpose, and happiness. There is no research to support that these are life's five basic needs. Based on our combined 140 years of experience and common sense, we suggest that they are basic needs. Further, they do coincide with Maslow's hierarchy of needs: his physiological and security needs are met by control; his social and self-esteem needs are met by caring and happiness; his self-actualization needs are met by purpose. Central to these basic needs is control. Without control, a person can't achieve their purpose in life and happiness is elusive.

It could be argued that caring is more important than control. Ask yourself this question, "How would it feel one morning to wake up and realize that no one cared about you?" Which is more important, caring or control? We do not have an answer for that question. We will let our readers ponder it. We do suggest that when caring, control, purpose, and happiness are not present, the desire for **life** is not very strong, and a person with this profile is a potential candidate to do something tragic. Suicide, taking a gun to school and shooting, drugs, alcohol, truancy, and gangs are all possibilities.

By creating a high-performing school culture, these five basic needs are being met. Through use of the redirects, students are asked to control their own and each other's behavior. When other students help them with homework so that they don't get redirects, or correct them for misbehavior, both **control** and **caring** needs are being met. It also gives them a **purpose**, and that is to get the reward for good behavior. If students' caring, control, and purpose needs are being met, their **happiness** needs will also be met. They enjoy **life** and actually enjoy going to school.

Suggested Plan for Phase I

There should be a weekly or daily reward for staying under the targeted number of redirects, or reminders. This is the peer group's motivator, and this can be done by classroom, team, grade level, or the whole school. There should also be an end-of-report-period reward for all students who have stayed under the targeted number of violations. This is the individual's motivator. There should be an individual daily punishment for anyone who exceeds a set number of redirects. There should be some way for students to redeem themselves if they have lost the privilege of taking part in the end-of-report-period reward.

This creates a two-pronged approach for shaping desirable student behavior: (1) all students are encouraged to control their own behavior so that they can eat lunch with their friends and participate in the end-of-report-period reward and (2) they are encouraged to correct other students' misbehavior and to work with other students to receive the peer group reward. The result is a plan to reward desirable behavior and extinguish undesirable behavior.

Some people might be opposed to giving rewards because they feel students should do what they are supposed to do because it is the right thing to do and not because there is a reward. This process complies with reward theory because the reward is intermittent and it is received by a group of students (the peer motivator). Another reward is given at the end of the report period for those (the individual motivators) that earned it. Students do not receive a reward each time they do something they are supposed to do.

Implementation of Phase I should occur at the school level, but if school officials want to try a gradual approach, they could ask some teachers to try it in their individual classrooms. Another alternative would be to start with office referrals, tardies, or absences or any combination of these. School officials should establish the benchmark and have a clearly visible indicator of progress toward achieving that benchmark.

One such indicator is a thermometer-like poster near the entrance. Everyone in the school is aware of the progress or lack thereof in reaching the established mark for the group reward. If the benchmark is reached, the entire school gets the reward. Whether the weekly or daily approach is used can be determined by school officials. However, we believe the daily benchmark for redirects is the most effective approach.

The role of the entire faculty and staff should also be considered! We suggest that the cooks, custodial staff, secretaries, and all other noncertified staff be involved in the process of counting redirects. Whether and when to involve the bus drivers is a judgment call, but eventually, we believe they should also be involved. Another judgment call is when to use failure to do homework as a redirect. However, when to involve all noncertified is critical. They need to feel a part of the team and this is the easiest way to do it. Let them count redirects and they will know that they are just as important as the teachers and administration when it comes to having a role in improving student behavior.

Implementation of Phase I gives all school stakeholders a clear vision of all the components of the mission. They are the following:

- to give control without giving it up;
- implement servant leadership;
- implement the redirect process to reduce student misbehavior;
- create a cooperative learning environment; and
- meet the five basic needs of all involved personnel.

There is a strong need to move away from using letter grades and punishment as motivators, as is the practice in traditional schools. In enlightened traditional schools, it is every individual for himself or herself. Each individual accrues his or her own rewards, creating a great deal of competition. According to Kohn (2014), cooperation is a better educational environment than competition. He believes that competition creates a rivalry and mistrust that undermines excellence for everyone involved. It pits students against each other. He believes that cooperation would create a community environment where students work to help each other instead of competing with each other.

In the high-performing school culture, the reward goes to a group of students, creating cooperation. The end result tends to be a community where students work together as citizens for a common reward. School culture and climate are improved which encourages student success, improved test scores, and reduced dropout rates. It is a collaborative environment where faculty and students work together. In his research, Gruenert (2005) concluded that a collaborative culture is the best setting for student achievement. He warned that school leaders should not "lose sight of the bigger picture of creating the social conditions necessary for student and teacher success" (p. 51). We are not advocating to get rid of competition, grades, and punishment in the high-performing school. We are instead advocating that cooperation is more important than competition.

A positive culture of control is created, and at the same time, a character education program that requires no curriculum or extra effort on the part of the faculty is established. The high-performing school culture creates an environment where students and faculty have an opportunity to model responsibility, dependability, accountability, perseverance, courtesy, kindness, compassion, respect, cooperation, and tolerance.

In the traditional school, which represents most schools, there are few opportunities for students to practice good citizenship because they are being controlled by the administration and faculty. They are told what the rules and consequences are, and they must comply or face reprimand. In the enlightened traditional school, they are encouraged to control themselves, but it is a highly competitive environment. There is no incentive for students to help each other.

Many schools are the antithesis of what is required for the future of a successful society. Graduates are needed who have had opportunities to help each other, who have had experience working in a community of other citizens, who believe that they make a collective difference, who have experienced the rewards of working together, and who are willing to step forward and intervene when needed. This does not occur in the traditional or enlightened traditional school.

Many opportunities for this to occur are present every day in a high-performing school culture. If we want good citizens, we must change the control culture that exists in most schools and create an environment that is more representative of what is expected when they graduate. We expect them to vote, we expect them to play an active role in their community, we expect them to be good parents (to serve their spouse and children), and we expect them to step forward when they see something that is wrong. If we maintain these expectations, we must create opportunities for them to practice these behaviors in the school setting.

There is more to school than academics. It should be a cocoon for creating citizens who are concerned not only for their own welfare, but also for the welfare of the rest of the society in which they live. We need to graduate students who are servant leaders as opposed to self-serving ones. That is not occurring, as evidenced by a high dropout rate and the number of citizens who are actively involved in the political process (only 50% of Americans vote). While the concept of a high-performing school does work, it is even more effective if the entire faculty comes across as servant leaders and not as self-serving ones, and that is the subject of the next chapter.

CONCLUSION

Implementation of Phase I will impact the following three of the six areas that impact test scores.

- improve **discipline** and time lost correcting student misbehavior by 75%
- improve **school culture and climate**
- meet the **needs** of students, faculty, and the administration

The other three areas are overuse of control, lack of parent involvement, and poor levels of openness and trust. These areas will be addressed in the remaining chapters.

REFERENCES

Beane, A. L. (2009). *Bullying prevention for schools: A step by step guide for implementing a successful anti-bullying program.* San Francisco: Jossey Boss.

Beane, A. L., & Bulach, C. R. (2009, September). *Tips for helping children who are bullied. School Climate Matters,* The Center for Social and Emotional Education.

Berger, R. (2003). *An ethic of excellence: Building a culture of craftsmanship with students.* Portsmouth, NH: Heineman.

Bulach, C. R., & Malone, B. (1994). *The relationship of school climate to the implementation of school reform.* ERS SPECTRUM: Journal of School Research and Information. 12(4). 3–9.

Bulach, C. R., Malone, B., & Castleman, C. (1995). *An investigation of variables related to student achievement.* Mid-Western Educational Researcher. 8(2). 23–29.

Bulach, C. R., Fullbright, P. J., & Williams, R. (2003). *Bullying behavior: What is the potential for violence at your school?* Journal of Instructional Psychology. 30. 156–164.

Bulach, C. R. *"An analysis of the West Virginia character education initiative."* A presentation at the Character Education Partnership 13th National Forum on 10-27-2006 at Arlington, VA.

Colombi, G., & Osher, D. (2015). *Advancing school discipline reform.* Education Leaders Report. 1(2), National Assessment of State Boards of Education.

Dearborn, G. (2015, September). *Compassionate discipline: Dealing with difficult students.* Association for Middle Level Education (AMLE) Magazine.

Gray, P. (2009, November, 2nd). *Why Students Don't Like School? Well, Duhhh.* Psychology Today.

Gruenert, S. (2005). *Correlations of collaborative cultures with student achievement.* NASSP Bulletin. 89(645). 43–55.

Joftus, S. (2002, September). *The challenge: Academic failure among secondary students. Every Child A Graduate.* Washington, DC: Alliance for Excellent Education.

Kohn, A. (2014). *The myth of the spoiled child:* Challenging the conventional wisdom about children and parenting. Boston: De Capo Press.

Kohn, A. (2006). *Beyond discipline: From compliance to community.* Alexandria, VA: Assn for Supervision & Curriculum Development.

Kohn, A. (2004). *Rebuilding school culture to make schools safer.* The Educational Digest. 70(3). 23–30.

Lewis, K. R. (August, 2015). *What if everything you knew about disciplining kids was wrong?* Mother Jones and the Foundation for National Progress.

Marzano, R. J., Marzano, J. S., & Pickering, D. J. (2003). *Classroom management that works: Research-based strategies for every teacher.* Alexandria, VA: Association for Supervision and Curriculum Development.

Maslow, A. H. (1943). *A theory of human motivation.* Psychological Review. 50(4) 370–96.

Nietzsche, F. (1910). "The will to power: An attempted transvaluation of all values. Books one and two." In Oscar Levy. *The complete works of Friedrich Nietzsche.* 14. Edinburgh and London: T.N. Foulis.

Office of the Press Secretary. (2011, March 10). President and First Lady Call for United Effort to Address Bullying. Retrieved 6-12-2015 from https://www.whitehouse.gov/the-press-office/2011/03/10/president-and-first-lady-call-united-effort-address-bullying.

Pearson, P. L. (2015). High school culture, graduation rates, and dropout rates. Doctoral dissertation, University of Southern Mississippi. Retrieved 6-12-2015 from http://aquila.usm.edu/dissertations/55/.

Sergiovanni, T., Starratt, R., & Cho V. (2013). *Supervision: A redefinition* (9th ed.). New York: McGraw-Hill.

Silva, P., & Mackin, R. A. (2002). *Standards of mind and heart: Creating the good high school.* New York: Teachers College Press.

Stetson, E. A., Hurley, A. M., & Miller, G. E. (2003). *Can universal affective education programs be used to promote empathy in elementary children?* Journal of Research in Character Education. 1(2). 129–147.

Chapter 2

A Four-Step Process for Identifying and Reshaping the Culture of a School (Phase II)

In chapter 1 we described Phase I in school reform. It addressed three the areas that impact test scores: **discipline** and time lost in the instructional process; **school culture and climate**; and the **five basic needs** of students and faculty. However, implementing a change in the control culture is only one phase of this comprehensive reform. Creating a high-performing culture, which is distinctly different from that in most schools, also requires a different kind of leadership, both for administrators and teachers.

The leadership style needed for implementing this type of school culture has been described by Greenleaf (1996) and Blanchard and Hodges (2003) as servant leadership. In addition to implementing Phase I of the process, it is also necessary to identify and reshape the existing culture of the school (Phase II). First, we will describe what is meant by servant leadership and the need for a comprehensive reform. Then we will describe each of the four steps for identifying and reshaping a school's existing culture. How to come across as a servant leader will be a part of this process in Phase II.

SERVANT LEADERSHIP

Greenleaf is the founder of the Servant as Leader concept. His original 1970 work is a series of essays. The Robert K. Greenleaf Center was founded in 1985 to promote the servant leadership concept. In a 1998 publication, he wrote that a true leader must first become a servant. A leader who is a servant realizes that his or her first priority is the needs of the people being led. Keep in mind, however, that the needs of the organization must also be met.

An analogy of the apple tree can be used to illustrate this point. Think of the tree as the organization and the apples as the people. There can be no apples without the tree. This is also true of most organizations. If the organization is not productive, it will not survive, and the staff will be jobless. A servant leader has to keep the needs of both in balance to maintain a high-performing school.

A principal must always balance the needs of the people (staff and students) and the needs of the organization (tasks and goals). Principals see this clearly as they accommodate teacher requests for teaching assignments, planning periods, and classroom assignments. The tasks must meet the needs of the organization. Not all teachers can have the last period for planning or teaching advanced placement classes.

This is an example of the balls the principals must juggle in meeting the needs of the staff and the organization. However, this can create a problem for principals. In meeting the needs of the organization, the principal can appear self-serving. In this book, the authors show how to be a servant leader while at the same time meeting the needs of the staff and the organization.

A servant leader, through the creative use of power and authority (the subject of chapter 4), creates a culture where there is a feeling of community openness, trust, and cooperation. There should be opportunities for students and faculty to assume responsibility and improve personal abilities.

Greenleaf's (1996) ideas about leadership are expanded on by Blanchard and Hodges (2003). They take Greenleaf's concept and use the life of Jesus Christ to describe servant leadership. They maintain that he was a great leader because he came to serve. They state that "in his instructions to his disciples on how they were to lead, Jesus sent a clear message to all those who would follow Him that leadership was to be first and foremost an act of service" (p. 12). Lest the reader reject the concept of servant leadership because of their beliefs and the mention here of Jesus Christ, please keep in mind some of Blanchard's and Hodges's other thoughts on leadership.

They maintain that our public leadership style determines whether others will follow. If followers perceive that the leader's behavior and habits are self-serving, as opposed to the benefit of those who are being led, there will be resistance to that person's leadership. They maintain that many leaders are self-serving and addicted to power and recognition.

The concept of servant leadership has been around for more than 30 years, yet it has received little attention from most educational leaders. Is it possible that most leaders are self-serving and more concerned for their own welfare than for the people in the organization they are leading? According to Blanchard and Hodges (2003), "The reality is that we are all self-serving to a degree because we came into this world with self-serving hearts" (p. 22).

Is this why there is so much resistance to change and reform in education? Is this why improving the quality of instruction and improving test scores is so difficult? Is this why the No Child Left Behind law was passed? Greenleaf (1998) discussed the role of listening, caring, trust, and the appropriate use of power and authority for servant leadership. However, they do not give a clear vision of how to operationalize the concept and create such a culture.

Such a culture is required for a high-performing school. In a high-performing school, servant leadership is practiced, not only by the principal, but also by the teachers and students. For example, the principal shares his or her power and authority with the teachers, and the teachers share power with their students. This creates a culture where everyone has maximum opportunities to grow, mature, and become responsible, not because someone is supervising them, but because it is the right thing to do.

The end result is a school culture where all faculty, students, and parents are focused on being of service to each other. How can such a culture be created? In chapters 1–5, the authors explain four distinct phases for creating such a culture. Any of these phases can help create such a culture, but when all four phases are implemented, a high-performing school, dedicated to the service of others, is more likely to occur. In this chapter, we describe Phase II of the process. Creating a culture for a high-performing school will address the concerns of many critics of today's educational system.

THE NEED FOR A COMPREHENSIVE SCHOOL REFORM

Quint (2006) summarized lessons learned from three models of school reform and discussed the importance of caring learning communities for students. One of the findings is that many schools are too large and must be broken up into smaller learning communities so that students will feel that their teachers know and care about them. Quint also discussed the need for and difficulty of a comprehensive school reform and the resistance to change.

A 2007 report by the National Center on Education and the Economy (NCEE) also called for a comprehensive school reform. The report stated that there is a growing mismatch between the type of students our schools are producing and the needs of the economy. The report detailed a series of initiatives designed to reform the way schools operate. In an earlier statement by Marc Tucker, who is the architect of the report, "This country is cooked if we don't make a vast improvement in the outcomes for our kids" (Olszewski and Rado, 2006, p. 10A).

In a later report in 2014, the NCEE focused on test scores and teachers. A summary of the report is that the current system has failed to improve the performance of the at-risk students it was designed to help. Further, it has alienated teachers and created a school culture and climate that is not inviting for future teacher prospects.

There have been many other reports that called for school reform. For example, the National Governors Association hosted an unprecedented two-day National Education Summit on High Schools in 2005. It was attended by 45 governors, educators, and business leaders. The purpose of the summit was to address the nation's alarming dropout rate and the fact that most students leave high school without the skills necessary for success in college or the workplace. In the opening session of the summit, Bill Gates stated that the nation's high schools were obsolete (Omear, 2005).

Steinberg, Johnson, and Pennington (2006), in a report for the Center for American Progress, wrote that it is time for an aggressive national effort to pursue a high-school reform effort that addresses two needs: (a) a reduction in the dropout rate and (b) higher standards. According to the report, one-third of all high-school students do not graduate. Allowing more than 1 million students a year to drop out without a diploma is too great a cost. Further, according to the report, the federal government needs to pass a Graduation Promise Act that would fund the implementation of proven strategies for keeping students in school and improving student achievement.

A Building a Grad Nation 2015 report on graduation rates indicated an improvement, but also noted that subgroups are the ones most affected by graduation rates. They found that minorities, ethnicities, family income, students with disabilities, and limited English proficiencies are most likely to drop out (Balfanz, Bridgeland, Bruce, and Fox, 2013).

In a 2013 Building a Grad Nation report, Colin Powell wrote the following in an opening letter:

> We need to sound a stronger alarm. We are running out of time to close large and lingering gaps in graduation rates among different student populations. While progress is substantial in many areas of the country, the number of non-graduates remains disturbingly high for students of color, students from low-income families, and young people with disabilities. Even among those young people who graduate, too many are poorly prepared for college and an increasingly demanding workforce. (p. 3)

The 2015 report mentions dropout factory high schools where the enrollment in the twelfth grade is 60% less than that in the ninth grade. These schools tended to be inner city schools with a large percentage of minorities and low-income students. The report does indicate that progress is being made toward a 90% graduation rate by 2020 (DePaoli, Fox, Ingram, Maushard, Bridgeland, and Balfanz, 2015).

In a press release on January 12, 2015, Carmel Martin, executive vice president for Policy at the Center for American Progress, issued the following statement after Secretary of Education, Arne Duncan, announced his principles for a reauthorized Elementary and Secondary Education Act. "A high-performing public school system is essential for our future economic competitiveness and the foundation of our nation as a place of opportunity for all." He also indicated that the focus has to be on school improvement and not on test scores.

However, there is a great deal of resistance to Duncan's leadership and his Common Core. In logging on to the website of Truth in American Education (January 2015), there were five articles where states are asking to opt out of Common Core standards. It seems that everyone has an issue with our schools and no one has a solution to fix the problem.

The Koret Task Force (2003) also reaffirmed the lack of progress in school reform. Further, according to the *Time* magazine cover article "Dropout Nation" (Thornburgh, 2006) and the follow-up Oprah Winfrey poll, "55% of Americans are dissatisfied with public schools and 61% think public schools are in a crisis" (Amos, 2006, p. 3). Boone, Hartzman, and Mero (2006), in trying to address the need for reform, wrote, "Breakthrough High Schools: Lessons Learned." However, a specific plan on how to create such a school was not given. Clearly it is time to come up with a school reform that will address this need and reduce resistance to change.

Peterson, P. E. (November 12th, 2014) wrote in *Education Next* that any reform will likely be met with resistance by teacher organizations like the NEA and the AFT. While progress is being made to reform schools and improve graduation rates, according to Grad Nation reports, the improvements are slow in coming and, in many cases, they are being resisted by faculty.

The reform we propose will not be met with resistance because it does not change what teachers teach or the way they teach. It changes the way faculty and students are treated. It changes the interpersonal relations. Those changes address six of the causes of poor test scores: **discipline, basic needs, school culture and climate**, the use of power, parent and community involvement, **and levels of openness and trust**. Chapter 1 addressed four of these needs. What is described in this chapter will improve levels of **openness and trust**.

Chapter 1 describes one of the four phases needed for a comprehensive approach to school reform. The remainder of this chapter and chapters 3 through 5 is devoted to describing a clear process for creating a culture and climate for a high-performing or "Citizenship School."

HOW DOES OUR REFORM ADDRESS THIS
NEED FOR A COMPREHENSIVE REFORM?

In this book, the authors unveil a comprehensive approach to school reform that reduces resistance to school reform and increases the likelihood of creating a caring learning community. Creating a high-performing school is an organizational approach to school reform that creates a distinctly different school culture and climate than can be found in nearly all existing schools.

Based on research (described in chapter 1), students like being part of such a culture. They have some control over their environment and are part of a caring learning community. This will result in higher test scores, a lower dropout rate, and reduced bullying behavior. Further, the type of student produced by this school environment should be a more productive citizen. How can a school leader implement this approach without encountering resistance to this change?

Organizational theorists like Bennis (2009) and others are aware that a leader who attempts a reform or change is in for a struggle because the system will resist the change. The secret of successful leadership is to identify the existing culture and reshape it to minimize the struggle. Principals who fail to identify the existing culture before introducing change will meet with resistance.

It is Bulach's belief, based on his 14 years' experience as a superintendent, that a principal must identify the existing culture. If not, the odds are 50/50 that in two or three years, the system will win the struggle, and the principal will be searching for another job. Consequently, a major task in Phase II for creating the culture for a high-performing school is to identify and reshape the existing culture. According to Peterson and Deal (2002):

> Every principal should take some time to decipher the symbolic glue that holds a school together. The easiest time to do this is when the principal is new and not yet indoctrinated into existing mores and norms. But it can also be done by any veteran who makes the commitment. (p. 133)

Bulach (2001a) created a four-step process for doing this that also lays the groundwork for the introduction of the servant leadership concept. The first step is to identify the existing culture described by Deal and Peterson (2009) as a set of expectations that affects the daily interactions of people and provides meaning and purpose for what happens in the work setting.

THE EXPECTATIONS DIAGNOSIS: FACULTY INPUT (STEP 1)

While there are other techniques for identifying a school's culture, such as surveys and outside consultants, a technique Bulach calls "the expectations diagnosis" is preferred (Step 1). This technique requires little time and can be accomplished at the first faculty meeting of the school year. The expectations diagnosis requires that all faculty members receive three 3 x 5 index cards. They should write an expectation they have of the principal on each card.

These expectations can be how they want to be treated and/or the rules they want enforced. Writing one expectation per card allows for easy sorting. More or fewer than three cards can be used, but based on past experience with this process, three cards work best. An explanation of why this information is needed and how it will be used should be made since trust has likely not been established.

The principal should explain to the faculty that one of the duties of the leader is to enforce rules and policies for both students and faculty. While the rules and policies for students tend to be clear, the ones for faculty are likely to be more flexible and subject to interpretation. Explain that faculty input on the rules and expectations is needed in order for the school to function at peak efficiency. The principal should clarify how the 3 x 5 cards will be used and that one expectation per card allows them to be quickly sorted into common groups.

This input allows teachers' values and beliefs to be included in decisions that affect them, which is important for empowerment and in gaining trust with staff. Teachers who are empowered will feel that they have a voice in how the school operates, and there will be less disenchantment with policies and rules that affect them. Obviously, teachers can't decide things such as the pay scale or school calendar, but they can have a voice in school regulations such as dress down day, staff parking, and so forth.

Once the cards are sorted into piles, it will be easy to identify the values, beliefs, or culture regarding the type of leadership the faculty prefers. A list of the 10–15 most frequently mentioned expectations should be compiled. This list is then given to faculty, and they are asked to rank items from most important to least important. Based on the rankings, the faculty's expectations regarding leadership can be determined. These expectations are shared with the faculty, and thus, what was previously a hidden culture becomes a shared one.

What tends to emerge is a list of rules/expectations regarding faculty and administrator interactions. Research indicates that some likely rules/expectations are as follows:

- faculty should be involved in the decision-making process;
- all faculty should be treated the same;
- the principal must be consistent in disciplining students who are sent to the office;
- rules should be enforced;
- the principal should not have favorites;

- the principal should be visible; and
- the principal should work with individuals who violate rules of the school or district instead of berating the entire faculty at a staff meeting.

This process creates a subtle shift in power, as it puts the principal in the position of enforcing the expectations of the faculty rather than those of the principal. The principal is serving the faculty, and servant leadership is in place. For example, if a faculty member is routinely late for work, he or she is informed that the faculty expects the principal to enforce the rules. One of those rules is that they must be on duty at 7:30 a.m. Instead of having to use position, reward, and coercion power to enforce the rules, the principal can now use information and moral power.

"Moral power" is a term used by Sergiovanni and Starratt (2013) and Bulach (1999) to describe a form of power that motivates others to do what they are supposed to do because it is the right thing to do. The fact that the faculty has set the rules and expectations creates a very different power relationship. Moral power is a form of power that can never be used too often, whereas position power, if used too often, tends to lose its force. However, if moral power does not work, the principal must use position power to enforce the rules. The nine forms of power and their use and misuse are described in chapter 4.

There is no best way to conduct an expectations diagnosis. Some principals may prefer to set aside five to ten minutes at the start of the first faculty meeting. Others may want to collect expectations at the end of the day. A word of caution: We suggest that this should be done as a spontaneous expectations diagnosis, where teachers can think and respond independently. If the teachers are allowed to get together and discuss, the individual values and beliefs may not be identified.

Keep in mind that the rest of the staff, that is, custodians, paraprofessionals, cooks, bus drivers, and so forth, also have expectations that will shape the culture of the institution. The same process should be used with those individuals. It is suggested that different colored index cards be used to assist with the sorting process. The expectations of the nonteaching staff are likely to be different from those of the certified faculty. The colored cards allow each group's expectations to be identified.

According to Barth (2002), a leader cannot reshape a school's culture until the existing culture is identified. This process is the first step in identifying and reshaping the existing culture, and it initiates the concept of servant leadership. Reshaping the culture occurs because the leader has listened to the faculty/staff and laid the groundwork for the development of trust.

Greenleaf (1998) and Blanchard and Hodges (2003) have discussed the importance of listening in servant leadership. Greenleaf believes that the act of listening builds strength in others because their needs are being met when listening occurs. Listening is also an activity that conveys that the leader cares (one of the basic needs) about the faculty's opinions, beliefs, and values. It also expresses that the leader is open to changing their leadership style to meet faculty expectations better.

Openness and trust are clearly intertwined (Bulach and Peterson, 2001). Once faculty perceive that the principal is there to serve their interests and that he or she cares and is open to them, the foundation for trust has been formed. The existing culture cannot be reshaped without some level of trust between the principal, faculty, and staff.

Gibb (1978) described the importance of openness and trust for high-performing organizations. He maintains that as trust grows, people become more open and less fearful, and change is more likely to occur. He stated that schools with high levels of trust will quickly outperform schools with low levels of trust. He portrayed a school with low levels of trust as one where the principal comes in as an outsider and imposes his or her values on the faculty. This causes "a massive system defense that mobilizes counter energy" (p. 198).

Once a school leader decides that the faculty does not trust him or her, a more controlling form of leadership occurs that further mobilizes counter-energy. This causes more controlling and more counter-energy, and so the cycle of underperformance continues until the leader is replaced. In schools where there are high levels of trust, the use of authority and controlling forms of power (discussed in chapter 4) is curtailed because faculty and students are self-determined and intrinsically motivated.

While the expectations diagnosis sets the stage for faculty to trust the leader, it also conveys to the faculty/staff that the leader trusts them. Step 1 creates a process for openness and allows subordinates to set the parameters for the operation of the school. Based on our experience with this process, the rules and expectations of the faculty are going to be more stringent than the rules that would be set by the administration. The principal in such a setting is in a much more powerful position than if he or she were enforcing her or his own rules.

THE EXPECTATIONS DIAGNOSIS: STUDENT INPUT (STEP 2)

Step 2 is the same process repeated by each teacher with their students. Students can be asked to write three expectations they have of their teachers. Today's classrooms have Latinos, students of color, Orientals, poor socio-economic and well-to-do socioeconomic students. Having some idea of the expectations of this mix of cultural backgrounds is very helpful in developing good relationships with students.

The same process should also be used to establish classroom rules. Students should be given three 3 x 5 index cards and asked to list three rules that should govern behavior in the classroom. This causes a dramatic change in the culture of the classroom because the teacher has become a servant. As a servant of the students, the teacher is enforcing the students' rules rather than the teacher's. Please note that the focus for students is on "rules" whereas with faculty it is on "expectations."

Because there is only one rule on each card, they can quickly be sorted into common piles for identification purposes. A chart of the most frequently mentioned rules should be made. The chart should contain at least 10 rules. More can be added, but the more rules a teacher has, the more difficult enforcement becomes. If a teacher wants a rule that the students have not identified, that rule can be included. One rule that students often do not put on the cards is, "Turn in homework on time." The students will never know that the teacher put that rule on the chart.

The use of redirects, described in chapter 1, can now be used by the teacher. If a rule is being broken by a student, the teacher should look at that student, and wait several seconds for the students to take control and change that student's behavior. That wait time and look should not be counted as a redirect. In so doing, the teacher is meeting one of the five basic needs: **control**. The teacher is giving control to the students without giving it up. If the misbehavior is not corrected, the teacher takes control back and corrects the misbehavior.

The psychological shift when students break their own rules versus those of the teacher is another example of moral power versus position power. The students set the rules for the right kind of behavior in the classroom. All the teacher has to do is remind students of how to do things right versus using position power to make students do the right thing. For example, if the classroom chart of rules is posted and a student is violating rule 2, the teacher only has to announce that rule 2 is being violated (a redirect). All eyes in the classroom focus on the student breaking that rule, and normally the student violating the rule will stop violating it.

There have been teachers in the Indiana schools who used the redirects as a hammer to control the students. They became even more control-oriented than prior to implementing the redirects. The second they saw a student misbehaving, they signaled a "redirect." They did not give students a chance to correct their own behavior. That is an incorrect use of redirects. Teachers should give students a few seconds to correct their own behavior before counting misbehavior as a redirect.

Marzano, Marzano, and Pickering (2008) described the importance of classroom management. Their research shows that there is a 28% reduction in classroom disruptions and a 20% increase in achievement when classroom rules and procedures are effectively implemented. If students are involved in setting the rules, they will help the teacher enforce the rules.

The data from chapter 1 indicate that there can be a 75% or greater reduction in redirects if students are given some control over their own behavior. Students like the feeling and belief that they have some control over what happens in a classroom as opposed to the traditional setting where enforcing rules and procedures is the sole responsibility of the teacher. Their control needs are being met. The end result is a reduction in redirects, time off task, and an increase in student achievement.

By being open and listening to students, the teacher demonstrates that he or she cares about the students and lays the groundwork for trust to develop. According to Bulach, Brown, and Potter (1998) and Bulach (2001b), there are five sets of behaviors that create a caring learning environment. *They are:

- behaviors that reduce anxiety,
- listening behaviors,
- rewarding behaviors,
- recognition behaviors, and
- friendship behaviors.

*A survey has been created that measures these sets of caring behaviors. The survey can be used to measure a teacher's caring behaviors. (See Appendix B).

The importance of listening behaviors was further described in Bulach (2000), where he wrote:

"The willingness to listen conveys that teachers are open to students. Students perceive that teachers care and this causes them to be open to their teachers. This is the foundation for trust to develop. Rapport between teachers and students is necessary before they take the risk of being open to learning." Figure 2.1 is an illustration of how this process can work:

THE LEARNING PROCESS

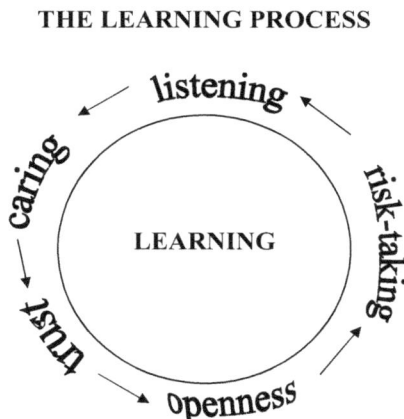

In order for learning to occur, the process begins with teachers showing students that they are willing to listen: This indicates to students that teachers care; students start trusting teachers, students are open and risk exposing themselves to the learning process. As students experience success, the cycle is repeated and students' motivation and learning increase. Granted there are other factors such as the teachers' personality, expertise, experience, subject content, etc., that are factors in the learning process. However, I believe that students will not risk learning until openness and trust are established. This basic human relationship between teachers and students starts with listening to students and showing them that you care. (p. 8)

The role of caring in creating a high-performing school culture can't be emphasized enough. According to Berger (2003): "Schools need to consciously shape their cultures to be places where it's safe to care, where it's cool to care" (p. 35). We believe that this feeling and belief that others care about you is one of the five basic human needs.

Maslow's hierarchy of needs (1954) identified five needs for learning or self-actualization to occur. They are security, safety, belonging, self-esteem, and self-actualization. The five basic needs we describe are similar, but different. For example, control is essential for Maslow's safety and security needs and caring meets the belonging and esteem needs. With those needs met, learning and self-actualization can take place. Using the learning process in Figure 2.1, a student's caring and control needs are met and learning will occur.

GETTING FEEDBACK ON FACULTY AND STUDENT EXPECTATIONS (STEP 3)

Step 3 in reshaping culture is to find out how teachers and students are responding to the school's leadership and how they are making adjustments as needed. Using a technique made popular by Kurt Lewin (1951) called "force-field analysis," there is a need to identify those forces "for" and "against" being the best possible principal or teacher. This should take place six to eight weeks after the start of the school year. Use index cards or a sheet of paper, and **have them complete the following two sentences as many times as they wish**. Reinforce that they can complete each sentence as often as they wish.

The principal is doing a good job because . . . (forces for)
The principal would do a better job if . . . (forces against)

This same force-field analysis process should be repeated by all of the teachers in their respective classrooms. Each teacher should identify those forces for and against being the best possible teacher.

(Name of teacher) is a good teacher because . . . (forces for)
(Name of teacher) would be a better teacher if . . . (forces against)

Again, this shows that the leader/teacher is willing to listen to faculty/students and is concerned about their welfare, cares about them, is willing to change the leadership style, and is there to serve. This is another way to give control (one of life's basic needs) without giving up control. This allows the formation of trust to continue, and valid feedback on the faculty's perception of the principal's leadership will be received. Based on the feedback, the principal/teacher can build on strengths or address things he or she needs to change. Identifying problems early in the school year allows the principal and teachers to be proactive rather than reactive when the problems surface later in the year.

According to Blanchard and Hodges (2003), one of the quickest ways to spot a self-serving leader as opposed to a servant leader is the way they handle feedback. The self-serving leader usually responds negatively because they think their leadership is not wanted, or they will rationalize why they are truly doing a good job as principal or teacher. The servant leader, however, welcomes feedback as an opportunity to provide better service to staff, students, parents, and the community.

A more formal approach for the principal to getting feedback and assessing their leadership is the leadership behavior survey. The survey measures behaviors in five areas that have allowed principals to create a positive supervisory climate or caused them to create a negative one (Bulach, Boothe, and Pickett, 2006). The five areas are the following: human relations, trust, instructional leadership, control, and conflict. Through the use of the survey, faculty members describe their perceptions of how their principal practices 49 leadership behaviors* that have been identified as important for a positive supervisory climate. Based on the data, the principal can identify strengths and weaknesses in these five supervisory areas.

The concept of servant leadership and the creation of a culture for a high-performing school must permeate the school. The principal asking the teachers and the teachers asking the students "How am I doing?" demonstrates that the leaders care and are there to serve. The same process could be extended to the rest of the staff, for example, secretaries, cafeteria workers, custodians, and so forth. This creates a culture of openness and risk-taking, both of which facilitate the development of trust (Bulach, 1974).

*The behaviors measured by this survey can be seen in appendix A.

ASSESSING A SCHOOL'S CULTURE AND CLIMATE (STEP 4)

The final step is assessing the climate and culture of the school four to six weeks prior to the end of the school year. This can be done through a formal or an informal survey. If an informal survey is chosen, the same force-field analysis process used to garner feedback on leadership style can be used. The two sentences faculty can complete as many times as they want are:

I like working at this school because . . .
I would like working at this school better if . . .

The same process could be used for students and parents,
using a variation of the two sentences. For example,
I like going to this school because . . . (students)
I would like going to this school better if . . .
I like sending my child to school because . . .
I would like sending my child to school better if . . . (parents).

If a formal survey is desired, the Association for Supervision and Curriculum Development, the National Association of Secondary School Principals, the National Association of Elementary School Principals, or the American Association of School Administrators can be contacted for information about surveys. Another source for school climate surveys is the National Center for School Climate at http://www.schoolclimate.org/. Definitions of culture and climate differ widely, and in some cases are used synonymously. However, they are distinctly different. This difference can be described by using the analogy of an iceberg.

Climate is the part of an iceberg that is easily seen above the water, and culture is the part of the iceberg below the water. The section below the water can't be seen, but it is there. The segment of the iceberg above the water can't exist without the part below the water. Similarly, the climate (what can be seen in a school) cannot exist without the underlying culture (what can't be seen).

This is a causal relationship: The underlying belief and value system (culture) results in the behavior seen in the organization (climate). Bulach, Malone, and Castleman (1995) described culture and climate as those psychological (culture) and institutional variables (climate) that give an organization its personality.

While there are instruments that measure culture or climate, we are not aware of one that measures both organizational variables. One instrument[1] that measures both was used by Bulach, Berry, and Williams (2001). The culture variables are group openness, trust, cooperation, and atmosphere.

This part of the survey provides data about how receptive people are, how trusting people are, how much individuals are willing to work together, and how much people care about one another. The climate variables are discipline, leadership, instruction, expectations, sense of mission, time on task/assessment, and parent involvement. These are also the "effective school" variables.* This part of the survey provides data on the extent to which students obey rules, if the principal leads, how teachers teach, and so forth.

*Association for Effective Schools (http://www.mes.org/correlates.html).

The advantage of the formal survey is that it provides detailed information about a school's strengths and areas needing improvement. The data are quantitative and allow for comparisons of pre- and post-implementation data to measure the effectiveness of the school-improvement plan (SIP). The use of an outside consultant to generate the climate and culture profile also adds authenticity to the data. The disadvantage is that there are costs involved for surveys, computer scan forms, data analysis, and writing of the report.

The advantage of the informal survey is that it is quick, easy, and costs only the time needed to analyze and describe the data. Since the data are of a qualitative nature, it is more difficult to analyze and make comparisons to see if the culture and climate have improved as a result of the improvement plan. One method of measuring the effectiveness of the plan, when qualitative data are used, is to count the number of times the faculty identify something they like about the school (forces for) and the number of times they identify something that would cause them to like the school better (forces against). If the plan has worked, the post-SIP data should have an increase in the number of things they liked (forces for) about the school and a decrease in the number of items they did not like (forces against).

CONCLUSION

School principals must identify the existing culture if they wish to introduce the servant leadership approach. They also have to change the culture that operates in most classrooms. This can happen if leaders and teachers become more servant-leadership-oriented. They must create conditions where the followers/subordinates create the rules and policies and the leader enforces them. The faculty and students identify the culture they want in the school and the principal and teachers help create and reshape it into a healthy learning environment. This continues the process of changing the control culture described in chapter 1.

Receiving early feedback on the supervisory climate created by the administration and teachers is important in avoiding more serious problems that could occur if one waits for end-of-year feedback. The overall culture and climate that have been created in the school also need to be analyzed and a plan implemented to improve it (the subject of chapter 3). These are proactive techniques that allow the reshaping of the culture and climate of a school where both the needs of the organization and the people within the organization are being met.

While the above process describes a plan for principals to use in identifying and reshaping the culture and climate of a school, the same process can be used by school superintendents and other administrators. The expectations of board members, teachers, and the administrative team can be ascertained using the same process. The supervisory climate of the superintendent can also be measured.

While the concept of servant leadership can exist at the building level and not at the district level, it would be fascinating to see what would happen if all central office and building personnel implemented this first phase to lay the groundwork for high-performing schools. Last, but not least, superintendents who ignore the climate and culture of the schools in their district are ignoring early indicators of schools that are headed for a decline in student achievement scores.

The call for school reform grows stronger with each report released, like the findings of the NCEE. It is time for a new approach, and we believe the methods outlined in this and other chapters will be beneficial for educators and will produce students who complete high school and become productive citizens. This reform addresses the basic needs of faculty and students, improves school culture and climate, improves discipline, and reduces time lost in the instructional process. It also addresses a fourth reason for poor test scores and that is the overuse of control which causes resistance and a lack of motivation. According to Lewis (2015) and Abrashof (2012), controlling behavior, rather than giving control, undermines motivation, autonomy, competence, and the development of healthy relationships. Techniques for giving control without giving up control have been described in this chapter. This reduces resistance and increases motivation for both teachers and students.

NOTE

1. Research manuscripts and reports in which the culture and climate survey and the leadership behavior survey mentioned in this chapter were used can be viewed and accessed at www.westga.edu/~cbulach. Behaviors measured by the survey can be seen in the Appendix of chapter 3.

REFERENCES

Abrashoff, M. D. (2012). *It's your ship: Management techniques from the best damn ship in the navy.* (10th ed.). Tempe, AZ: Warner Business.

Amos, J. (2006). *Oprah's on!: Oprah Winfrey, Bill and Melinda Gates, and more than 50 other partners announce national campaign on high school dropouts.* Alliance for Education: Straight A's. 6(8). 2–4.

Balfanz, R., Bridgeland, J. M., Bruce, M., & Fox, J. H. (2013). *Building a grad nation: Progress and challenge in ending the high school dropout epidemic.* Washington, DC: Civic Enterprises (http://civicenterprises.net).

Barth, R. (2002). *The culture builder.* Educational Leadership. 59(8). 6–11.

Bennis, W. (2009). *On becoming a leader.* Philadelphia, PA: Perseus Books Group.

Berger, R. (2003). *An ethic of excellence: Building a culture of craftsmanship with students.* Portsmouth, NH: Heineman.

Blanchard, K., & Hodges, P. (2003). *The servant leader.* Nashville, TN: J. Countryman.

Boone, E., Hartzman, M., & Mero, D. (2006). *Breakthrough high schools: Lessons learned.* Principal Leadership. 6(10). 51.

Bulach, C. R. (1974). *The relationship of openness, trust, and risk-taking.* Doctoral dissertation. University of Cincinnati, Cincinnati, Ohio.

Bulach, C. R. (1999). *Leadership techniques that control or empower subordinates: A new power typology.* Presentation at the Southern Regional Council of Education Administration, Charlotte, North Carolina. November 15, 1999.

Bulach, C. R. (2000). *How to show your TESOL students that you care!* TESOL in Action. 14(1). 7–9.

Bulach, C. R. (2001a). *A four-step process for identifying and reshaping school culture.* Principal Leadership. 1(8). 48–51.

Bulach, C. R. (2001b). *Now more than ever: Show kids you care!* The Education Digest. 67(3). 4–7.

Bulach, C. R., & Peterson, T. A. (2001, November). *Analyzing levels of openness and trust between principals and their teachers.* SRCEA 2001 Yearbook: Leadership for the 21st Century.

Bulach, C. R., Berry, J., & Williams R. (2001). *The impact of demographic factors on school culture and climate.* Paper presented at the Southern Regional Council of Educational Administrators. Jacksonville, Florida. November 3, 2001.

Bulach, C. R., Boothe, D., & Pickett, W. (2006). *Analyzing the leadership behavior of school principals.* CONNEXIONS. Retrieved October 25, 2006 from www.cnx.org/content/m13813/latest.

Bulach, C. R., Brown, C., & Potter, L. (1998). *Behaviors that create a caring learning community.* Journal of a Just and Caring Education. 4(4). 458–470.

Bulach, C. R., Malone, B., & Castleman, C. (1995). *An investigation of variables related to student achievement.* Mid-Western Educational Researcher. 8(2). 23–29.

Deal, T. E., & Peterson, K. D. (2009). *Shaping school culture: Pitfalls, paradoxes, and promises.* San Francisco: Jossey-Bass.

DePaoli, J. L., Fox, J. H., Ingram, E. S., Maushard, M., Bridgeland, J. M., & Balfanz, R. (2015). *Building a Grad Nation: Progress and Challenge in Ending the High School Dropout Epidemic.* Annual Update: 2015.

Gibb, J. R. (1978). TRUST: *A new view of personal and organizational development.* Los Angeles: Guild of Tutors Press.

Greenleaf, R. K. (1996). *On becoming a servant leader.* Somerset, NJ: John Wiley & Sons Inc.

Greenleaf, R. K. (1998). *The power of servant leadership.* San Francisco, CA: Berret-Koehler Publishers Inc. (Edited by Larry Spears).

Herszenhorn, D. M. (2006, December 12). "Back to drawing board on education?" *Atlanta Journal-Constitution.* p. A9.

Koret Task Force. (2003). *Are we still at risk.* Palo Alto, CA: Hoover Institute.

Lewin, K. (1951). *Field theory in social sciences.* New York: Harper & Row.

Lewis, K. R. (2015, August). *What if everything you knew about disciplining kids was wrong?* Mother Jones and the Foundation for National Progress.

Martin, C. (January 12, 2015) *Any rewrite must retain core focus on equity, School Improvement.* Washington, DC: Center for American Progress.

Maslow, A. (1954). *Motivation and personality.* New York: Harper and Row.

Marzano, R. J., Marzano, J. S., & Pickering, D. J. (2008). *Classroom management that works: Research-based strategies for every teacher.* Lebanon, IN: Merrill

National Center on Education and the Economy. (2007). *Tough choices or tough times: The report of the new commission on the skills of the American workforce.* San Francisco: John Wiley & Sons.

National Center on Education and the Economy. (2014, August). *NCEE proposes new system of accountability and professionalizing teaching.* (www.ncee.org/accountability).

Olszewski, L., & Rado, D. (2006, December 15). "Panel calls for radical reform of U.S. education." *The Chicago Tribune*, p. 10A.

Omear, J. (2005, February). *Leaders call for equity, rigor in the American high school.* News release from the National Governors Association. Retrieved 7-17-2015 from http://www.nga.org/portal/site/nga/menuitem.6c9a8a9ebc6ae07eee28a ca9501010a0/?vgnextoid=185f137945da2010VgnVCM1000001a01010aRCRD& vgnextchannel=759b8f2005361010VgnVCM1000001a01010aRCRD.

Peterson, K. D., & Deal, T. E. (2002). *The shaping school culture fieldbook.* San Francisco: Jossey-Bass.

Peterson, P. E. (2014, December 17). *Education Next.* Retrieved 7-16-2015 from http://educationnext.org/simply-forming-exploratory-committee-jeb-bush-places-school-reform-national-agenda/.

Quint, J. (2006). *Research-based lesson for high school reform: Findings from three models.* Principals Research Review. 1(3). 1–8.

Sergiovanni, T., & Starratt, R. (2013). *Supervision: A redefinition (9th ed.).* New York: McGraw-Hill.

Steinberg, A., Johnson, C., & Pennington, H. (2006). *Addressing America's drop-out challenge: State efforts to boost graduation rates require federal support.* Washington, DC: Center for American Progress.

Thornburgh, N. (2006, April). *Dropout nation.* Time Magazine. 167(16). 31–40.

Truth in American Education. (2015, January). *Fighting to stop the Common Core State Standards, their Assessments and Student Data Mining.* Retrieved 7-15-2015 from http://truthinamericaneducation.com/.

Chapter 3

Implementing a Plan to Improve the Climate and Culture of the School

The control culture and the system of redirects should be firmly established by this time. The groundwork should have been laid for improving the culture of the school, and servant leadership should be in place at the school and classroom level. The values and beliefs of the teachers and students governing human interactions should have been identified through the "expectations diagnosis." Administrators and teachers should have received feedback on how their leadership is being accepted by subordinates.

According to Danielson (2002), a culture of respect and responsiveness for clients is very important if school improvement is to take place. The four-step process for identifying and reshaping the culture of a school demonstrated to faculty and students that the leaders are listening and care about them. Administrators and faculty are still very much in control, but control has been shifted to faculty and students. Remember the earlier statement in chapter 1: People want to be in a highly controlled environment, but still want to have some control. A lack of control causes resistance and poor motivation.

The final step the authors describe in chapter 2 is collecting data on the culture and climate of the school. This is necessary for developing a school-improvement plan (SIP) for the next school year. The principal needs to explain to the faculty that the mission of the school is to improve the quality of instruction and create a caring learning environment. How the faculty will be involved in using this data is crucial for creating a vision to accomplish this mission. In this chapter, the authors explain how the faculty can be involved; how to analyze and utilize the data; and how to compare data before and after the implementation of the SIP.

Stolp and Smith (1995) discussed the principal's role in creating a vision for his or her school. They maintained that the principal should be a facilitator in the process and should not impose his or her own beliefs on the faculty.

This opinion is shared by others who have also written extensively on creating a vision for a positive organizational culture (Cunningham & Gresso, 1993; Fullan, 2009; Senge, 1990).

According to Stolp and Smith (1995), the characteristics of such a culture are as follows: "The organization's members must listen to one another, feel empowered to change the organization, have confidence in their ability to improve their performance, think critically and gather data about where the organization is at present, and hold strong convictions about the ideals that should guide their work in the future" (p. 69).

DECIDING HOW TO PROCEED

In the first part of Phase I, control is shifted to faculty and students, and conditions are created for improving levels of trust between the administration and teachers. This creates an environment for a positive organizational culture to develop. If levels of trust are to continue improving, teachers have to be involved in developing the improvement plan. According to King (2002), the role of principals has changed. Principals must develop the leadership capacity of teachers by involving them in the decision-making process, and they must provide opportunities for them to collaborate on school-improvement issues. According to Berger (2003), teachers on many school staffs feel no ownership beyond their classroom and they feel powerless to deal with the broad issues of school culture. Servant leadership has to be in place and the faculty should have input into the way the school is organized.

Teacher involvement in shaping a school's culture is often determined by how the school is organized. Danielson (2002) agreed with Berger and writes, "How a school is organized is a matter for the staff to determine, and a school's organization should reflect the staff's commitment to the success of all students" (p. 43). Granted, all schools have some preexisting organizational pattern, and this is a good time to involve the faculty and ask if the preexisting pattern can be improved. If teams, departments, or any other pattern is used to organize the school, it is time to gather feedback on that organization. The "force-field analysis" technique described by the authors in chapter 2 can be used as follows (complete the following two sentences as often as you wish):

The structure of organizing this school by (describe here—is it by grade level teams, departments, etc.) is good because . . .
The structure of organizing this school by (describe here) would be better if . . .

The next step is to appoint a committee to analyze the data on the culture and climate (chapter 2) and on the organizational structure. Keep in mind that the formation of a committee could have been done much earlier. When the committee is appointed is not crucial. However, how the committee is appointed is very important if the trust-building process is to continue.

APPOINTING THE COMMITTEE

The committee should consist of representatives from each group of the preexisting organizational structure. Care should be taken to ensure that all members of the faculty are represented by the committee. This includes both certified and noncertified faculty. If trust building is to continue, it is imperative that the faculty be allowed to decide who will represent their group on the committee. If the principal appoints members, this will come across as self-serving, and it is a clear signal to the faculty that the principal does not trust them.

According to Stolp and Smith (1995),

> Culture building is a process that cuts deeply into the fabric of people's relationships, their patterns of communication and interaction, and their regard for their own potential as well as that of the organization they serve. An excellent culture is the net result of the activities of individuals who are themselves, both on their own and as members of a work group, growing in identity, confidence, knowledge, cooperation, commitment, and respect. (p. 64)

In keeping with that philosophy, the principal must allow the faculty to select their own representatives and elect the chair. The principal should serve as a facilitator and nonvoting member. The principal also has to identify what the committee's role will be in the culture-improvement process. Will the committee have the authority to make decisions or only recommendations? If they have the authority only to make recommendations to the principal or site-based council, it should be made very clear. If they have the authority to make decisions, is that authority limited to the SIP? It is important that the members of the committee understand their role.

The first task of the committee is to elect a chair. The second task is to decide how decisions will be made. Will decisions be made by majority vote or consensus? If they will be made by consensus, the committee must decide what is meant by consensus. There are different levels of consensus ranging from "I have some reservations, but I will support the decision" to "I wholeheartedly agree with and support the decision." Getting everyone to agree could be very time consuming. A lower level of consensus might be more advisable.

The next task is to analyze the force-field analysis data on the school's pre-existing organizational structure. If the forces for or against indicate a need to change the organizational structure, the committee should review those forces and make the necessary recommendations or decisions. According to Marzano (2003), the governance or organizational structure is crucial for high-performing schools. Also according to Lunenburg and Ornstein (2012), the organizational structure should be such that all personnel in the school are included in some group, allowing for a communication network where there are no "isolates." An "isolate" is a person who is not connected to another person in the school organizational structure.

If all personnel in the school are connected to some group (no isolates), then everyone is in the communication loop, allowing all personnel to have input in the communication process. If, as a result of the committee's recommendation, the organizational structure is revised and new groups are created, the school-improvement committee should be expanded to include a representative from those groups. Once the committee is intact, has chosen a leader, and has reached consensus on how decisions will be made, the process of analyzing the culture and climate data collected in chapter 2 can begin.

ANALYZING THE DATA

In this section, the authors describe two different ways to view the data. One method is to look at data from a quantitative standpoint. This method assumes that a formal survey was used to collect the data. The other method looks at data from a qualitative standpoint and assumes that an informal survey was used to gather the data. Hopefully, the quantitative data have been depicted in a bar graph. Based on the scores, it is easy to identify the strengths and areas needing improvement. For example, if the Bulach (2002) Instructional Improvement Survey (IIS) were used, there will be scores (see Appendix C) for the four culture variables (group openness, trust, cooperation, and atmosphere), and scores for the seven climate variables (discipline, teaching, instructional leadership, expectations, sense of mission, assessment/time on task, and parent involvement).

The scores represented on the graph are the result of faculty responses to the behaviors that make up each of the four culture and seven climate variables (this graph compares scores from the previous year with changes in the current year's scores as a result of the SIP). Scores near or above 32 indicate areas of strength and those below 32 are areas that should be considered for improvement. Each variable or subscale is measured by eight (8) behaviors. An "agree" response is scored as a four (4), which would produce a score of

32 (4 x 8 = 32). A "disagree" response is scored as a two (2), which would produce a score of 16 (2 x 8 = 16). A "completely agree" response is scored as a five (5) producing a score of 40. The areas of openness and trust have more than eight (8) behaviors, but they have been mathematically controlled to be equal with the other subscales.

In order to determine why one area or variable is high or low, it is necessary to view a report (see Appendix D) that gives scores for each of the behaviors that operationalize that culture or climate variable. All of the items that measure a given variable are grouped for each of the 11 subscales. To the left of each item under the heading "average response" is the average score on that item. Scores of 4.0 or better indicate areas where performance is good and faculty "agree" that the behavior is present. Scores below 4.0 indicate areas that can be improved. Keep in mind that some (those italicized) items are reverse scored, for example, item 40. If it is below 4.0, then faculty agree with the negative statement and believe that morale is low.

Suppose, on the other hand, the committee chose a different quantitative survey to measure school climate, such as the Organizational Climate Description Questionnaire (OCDQ) and described by Hoy and Hoy (2006). This survey measures the behavior of the principal and teachers on six climate dimensions. The principal's style of interacting with others is measured as supportive, directive, or restrictive. The teachers' behavior is measured as collegial, intimate, or disengaged. Based on the scores from the survey, the behavior is coded as open, engaged, disengaged, or closed. Scores can be graphed to quickly see strengths and areas needing improvement.

If a quantitative survey is chosen to collect data on the school's climate or culture, there are a number of things to consider. One consideration is whether culture or climate data are wanted or if data on both are wanted. Another consideration is the length of the survey. The OCDQ is very short, with only seven responses, and takes faculty about five minutes to complete. The IIS has 96 behaviors and takes faculty about 30 minutes to complete. The OCDQ is a measure of seven broad categories of behavior, and the IIS measures 96 very specific behaviors. It has eleven categories of behavior and measures both culture and climate.

A number of other surveys that collect data on a school's culture and climate are described by Stolp and Smith (1995). However, a major consideration should be how helpful the data are in developing the SIP. For example, suppose there is a low score on the OCDQ for the climate variable organizational clarity. It tells you that this area needs to be improved, but it does not tell you what behaviors are causing this low score. How helpful is this score in developing the SIP? On the other hand, if there is a low score on the IIS for the climate variable sense of mission, there are scores on eight behaviors that make up this variable. By looking at the scores for each behavior that make up this variable, the committee would have some guidance in developing a plan to improve scores related to sense of mission.

The above comparison is designed to provide the reader with some things to consider when a decision is made on selecting a survey instrument for the collection of climate and/or culture data.

If a qualitative survey such as the force-field analysis were to be used to collect the data, the task of analysis becomes a little harder. For example, if there are 50 faculty members on the staff, there will be 50 sheets of paper to be analyzed for themes or repeatedly occurring behaviors. Often there will be a number of behaviors that say similar things, but the wording could be different. This requires some judgment to paraphrase what the central behavior might be. For example, there could be 20 "better if" comments about faculty meetings, but many of them say different but somewhat similar ideas. Analyzing all this data and writing the report for themes about the forces for and against a good school culture requires time and effort.

GETTING FEEDBACK FROM FACULTY ON HOW TO IMPROVE THE CLIMATE AND/OR CULTURE

The first step in getting feedback from the faculty on how to improve the climate and/or culture is to share the results of the quantitative or qualitative assessment. Based on the report, the strengths and areas needing improvement are identified. If the IIS were used to collect the data, it is recommended that one culture variable and one climate variable be identified as the two areas needing improvement. The reason for this recommendation is that the variables are all highly related. Bulach (2002) concluded, "The correlations for the 11 culture and climate factors tend to be very high. For example, the correlation between expectations and assessment/time on task has a correlation of +0.939" (p. 2).

Since the factors are highly correlated, any change in one will result in positive changes in the other factors. According to Reeves (2004), it is important that the SIP be successful. A focus on one culture and climate variable is more likely to accomplish success. The shotgun approach of developing a plan targeting all 11 variables is less likely to be successful because of lack of focus.

In selecting the culture and climate variables, group openness is almost always the culture variable with the lowest score and the lowest relationship with the other culture and climate variables. According to Bulach and Williams (2002), "The low correlations with openness are probably a result of the two dimensions measured by this factor. Openness has a telling and a listening dimension. Faculty can be very open on the telling dimension and closed on the listening dimension and vice versa. We believe this is the reason why correlations tend to be low for openness with the other factors" (p. 2). Past experience in working with more than 100 schools indicates that this culture variable should not be the variable targeted for improvement, even if it is the lowest score.

This recommendation is based on two reasons: (1) because of the low correlation with the other variables, a change in this variable will have less of an impact on the other variables and (2) because openness is the most difficult to change. Improving levels of group openness requires time for faculty to communicate and interact. Finding time for faculty to do this is very difficult because of schedules and the way schools are organized.

The behaviors associated with group atmosphere or group cooperation are much easier to change, and they have a strong relationship with the other variables. The school identified in Appendix C chose group atmosphere as the culture variable most needing improvement. They chose discipline as the climate variable most needing improvement. Based on their plan, they made significant improvements on these two variables and on all other culture and climate variables.

The overall culture and climate score went from 31.09 to 34.32 (p < 0.01). All other scores with the exception of group openness and cooperation improved to 32.00 or higher. A score of 32.00 is an agree response to imply that those behaviors occur. Scores approaching 40.0 are a strongly agree response.

With that as background, how can the entire faculty be involved in coming up with the SIP? The culture variable group atmosphere and the climate variable discipline will be used to explain this process. Following delivery of the report to the faculty, some form of the following instructions from the school-improvement committee (SIC) can be given:

We want your assistance in coming up with ideas on how to improve the behaviors associated with group atmosphere and discipline. We will give the chair of your group a packet of 3 x 5 or 4 x 6 index cards (size of the card is not important). Please review the eight behaviors associated with each of these variables, and pick two behaviors for each variable where you would like to see improvement. Write the behavior you would like to see changed on the card. Next write down one thing about that behavior that needs to improve or change to make you more positive about that behavior next year when the IIS is again administered.

Follow the same process for each card that you turn in to your group leader. You can use as many cards as you wish, but you are being asked to turn in at least four and identify two behaviors and two things you would like to see changed for each of the two variables targeted for improvement. Your leader will sort the cards for areas or behaviors where there is agreement regarding changes and write a report stating these changes. The report and the cards turned in by your group will be given to the School Improvement Committee.

When the report and cards are turned in to the committee, the cards can quickly be sorted into piles of common behaviors for each variable. Based on the reports and the data from the cards, the committee can identify which of the eight behaviors in group atmosphere and discipline will be targeted by the SIP.

Based on the reports and the data on the cards, there will also be a number of faculty suggestions regarding what needs to be changed to get a more positive score on that behavior. For example, the two group atmosphere behaviors targeted by the faculty of high-performing elementary school (see Appendix D) were the following:

• The administration shows favoritism to some constituents.
• Faculty and staff morale at this school is low.

Based on the data from the reports and cards, it was discovered that the principal was sending the same people to conferences and workshops. The committee recommended that teachers should have some input on who would represent them at conferences and workshops. While there were a number of other behaviors targeted by the SIP, this practice seemed to be causing the most problems. Scores on these two behaviors improved from 2.81 and 2.89 to 4.55 and 4.79, respectively.

When the cards and reports for discipline were analyzed, the following two behaviors were identified as those most in need of improvement:

• The procedure the administration has in place for office referrals and discipline is effective.
• The degree of communication with teachers about an office referral is appropriate.

Based on suggestions of what was needed to be changed for the faculty to be more positive about these two behaviors, a written communication system was developed for office referrals. Teachers were sometimes sending students to the office without a written note, and the principal was sometimes sending students back to the classroom without a written explanation of what had been done.

There was a lack of consistency with the way discipline was administered. Further investigation, as the SIP was implemented, revealed that teachers were sending students to the office for being disrespectful, disruptive, rude, uncooperative, and so forth. These were judgments and not specific behaviors which made it difficult for the principal to correct misbehavior.

The principal required that teachers write the specific behavior that caused the teacher to make that judgment about the student. The attitude adjustment or punishment that the principal used was much more specific and successful in correcting student behavior. Scores on these two behaviors improved from 2.76 and 2.95 to 4.24 and 4.32, respectively.

A similar process can be used if the qualitative survey is used to collect data about the climate and culture. The forces for and against should be reviewed for similarities. Suppose there were a number of against statements about faculty meetings. The 3 x 5 card system could be used as described previously. Each faculty member would write one statement on each card that, if changed, would make teachers more positive about faculty meetings.

The force-field analysis process, as mentioned by the authors in chapter 2, can also be used for parents and students to get their input about the forces for and against a high-performing school. Once parents and students identify the forces against, the same 3 x 5 card method can be used to get ideas on what needs to be changed. The concept of the caring learning environment, as illustrated by the paradigm in chapter 2, has to be reinforced for improved student achievement.

The use of the 3 x 5 card method shows that control is shifted and the leader is listening and cares about their feelings and thoughts. This leads to greater levels of openness, trust, risk-taking, and ultimately higher student learning and achievement. This entire process is enhanced if servant leadership is being practiced by the administration and faculty. An explanation of how students can become servant leaders can be found in chapter 5.

In addition to analyzing the data and using faculty feedback to develop the SIP, there are additional suggestions. Bulach and Berry (2001) investigated the impact of teacher experience on their perception of a school's culture and climate. Their research involved 1,163 teachers from 25 schools in Georgia.

They found that teachers with two to five years of experience had the poorest perception of a school's climate, followed by teachers with six to ten years of experience. They found that teachers who were in their first year were also more positive than teachers with two to ten years of experience. Additionally, teachers with the most experience had the most positive perceptions of their school's culture and climate.

One other finding was that female faculty members have a much more positive view of a school's culture and climate than male members. Consequently, the development of an SIP should give some thought to how faculty members with two to ten years of experience are being supported after their first year and further whether there are any differences that might exist between how male and female faculty members are treated. Finally, the SIP must be implemented, and periodic meetings of the SIP committee should occur to see how the plan is working and if changes need to be made. The force-field analysis process described earlier could be used to get feedback on the SIP by using: "The SIP is good because . . ." and "The SIP would be better if . . ."

COMPARING THE PRE-SIP DATA WITH POST-SIP DATA

The final step of Phase II is repeating the process for collecting the data that was used to develop the SIP and comparing it with the data after one year of implementation of the plan. An example of a pre- and post-comparison using the IIS can be found in Appendixes C and D. The use of the graph allows for easy detection of the success or lack of success of the SIP.

The use of the report for each of the behaviors permits school officials to determine what behaviors caused a culture or climate variable to change. Hopefully, the one culture variable and the one climate variable that were part of the SIP have improved. The SIP for the next school year should again include one culture and one climate variable. The selection of the targeted variables should be based on input from the entire faculty. Once the variables are selected, the 3 x 5 card method should again be used to get faculty input to help develop the SIP for the next school year.

If the qualitative force-field analysis is used to collect data, there are two ways to measure the success or lack of success of the SIP. The first comparison should be to look at the number of comments received about the targeted variable. If the targeted variable was faculty meeting, are there fewer comments in the "better if" or forces against section of the force field? Are there more comments about faculty meetings in the forces for section? For example, count the positive comments that faculty made in the pre-data (forces for), and compare that with the number of positive comments in the post-data.

Since the size of the faculty can change from year to year, the data used for the second comparison should be the number of positive comparisons for each faculty member. For example, if there are 50 faculty members and 150 pre-positive comments (3.0 per faculty member) about why they like working at the school and 200 post-positive comments (4.0 per faculty member), then the SIP has been successful.

The same process can be used to compare the pre-negative forces against with the post-negative forces. Hopefully, the number of times post-negative forces are mentioned per faculty member has decreased. The objective of the SIP should have been twofold: (a) to increase the number of times forces for are mentioned and (b) to decrease the number of times forces against are mentioned.

This process takes qualitative data and allows the leader to look at it from a quantitative approach as well. It is important to look at the frequency of positive and negative comments per person. This is particularly important if comparisons are made between student or parent data as their numbers can change a great deal from year to year.

CONCLUSION

The process described by the authors in chapter 3 completes Phase II. What we have described has many similarities to the five-stage process described by Cohen (2015). He describes the formation of the SIC, the collection of pre- and post-data, the importance of school climate, the action plan, the reevaluation of data, etc. Our process differs because of the emphasis on servant leadership, trust building, and shifting of the control culture concept.

The administration and faculty continue trust building by showing that they are willing to listen and that they care about the opinions of subordinates. The importance of teachers working together and the principal's role in focusing faculty attention on learning was supported by DuFour (2002). As stated by the authors in chapter 2, the mission of a high-performing school should be to focus on the continual improvement of instruction in a caring learning environment.

The vision of how to accomplish this mission can be illustrated by the learning paradigm described in chapter 2; that is, personal growth or learning starts with listening, and that leads to the belief that the leader cares. This creates an environment for servant leadership, openness, trust, risk-taking, and personal growth or learning.

Instructional improvement will occur because the following areas have been addressed: discipline, the five basic needs, culture and climate, control, and levels of openness and trust. If you recall from chapter 1, these are five of the six areas that impact test scores. The only one not addressed is parent and community involvement. That will be covered in chapter 5. More on how control can be shifted to faculty and students will be covered in the next chapter.

REFERENCES

Berger, R. (2003). *An ethic of excellence: Building a culture of craftsmanship with students*. Portsmouth, NH: Heineman.

Bulach, C. R. (2002). *An instrument that measures a school's culture and climate*. A presentation at the American Educational Research Association Conference, New Orleans, Louisiana, April, 2002.

Bulach, C. R., & Berry, J. (2001). *The impact of demographic factors on school culture and climate*. Resources in Education. (ED 462 744).

Bulach, C. R., & Williams, R. (2002). *The impact of setting and size on a school's culture and climate.* Resources in Education. (ED 467 672).

Cohen, J. (2015 Webinar, January 28th). *How to promote essential social, emotional, and intellectual competencies and create a climate for learning.* National School Climate Center.

Cunningham, W. G., & Gresso, D. W. (1993). *Cultural leadership: The culture of excellence in education.* Needham Heights, MA: Allyn & Bacon.

Danielson, C. (2002). *Enhancing student achievement: A framework for school improvement.* Alexandria, VA: Association for Supervision and Curriculum Development.

DuFour, R. (2002). *The learning-centered principal.* Educational Leadership. 59(8). 12–15.

Fullan, M. G. (2009). *The challenge of change: Start school improvement now!* Thousand Oaks, CA: Corwin Press.

Hoy, A. W., & Hoy, W. K. (2006). *Instructional leadership: A research-based guide to learning in schools.* Boston, MA: Allyn and Bacon.

King, D. (2002). *The changing shape of leadership.* Educational Leadership, 59(8), 61–64.

Lunenburg, F. C., & Ornstein, A. C. (2012). *Educational administration.* Belmont, CA: Wadsworth Publishing Company (6th ed.).

Marzano, R. J. (2003). *What works in schools: Translating research into action.* Alexandria, VA: Association for Supervision and Curriculum Development.

Reeves, D. B. (2004). *Accountability for learning: How teachers and school leaders can take charge.* Alexandria, VA: Association for Supervision and Curriculum Development.

Senge, P. M. (1990). *The leader's new work: Building learning organizations.* Sloan Management Review. 32(1). 7–23.

Stolp, S., & Smith S. C. (1995). *Transforming school culture: Stories, symbols, values, and the leader's role.* Eugene, OR: Eric Clearinghouse on Educational Management.

Chapter 4

Power and Authority

Nine Techniques for Motivating Faculty and Students (Phase III)

PHASE III
(When to Use the Freeing Forms of Power and
When to Use the Controlling Forms)

In chapter 1 (Phase I), we described the four different types of school cultures. How to implement the high-performing school culture by shifting control to faculty and students was also explained. In chapter 2 (Phase II), the authors described the importance of servant leadership. Various techniques for implementing servant leadership were also described. In chapter 3, suggestions were given on how to implement a plan for continuing to improve the culture and climate of a school. In chapter 4, the authors describe Phase III of the process for creating a high-performing school. The focus is on how school administrators, teachers, and faculty use power and authority to either give control or take control. All principals and teachers have a form of power called position power where they take control, and this gives them the authority to reward and/or punish faculty and students.

The way leaders use power to influence and motivate subordinates determines the kind of control culture that is created. According to McDowelle and Buckner (2002), "All the theories about how leaders use power, influence, and motivation are flawed. The most valuable thing we know about leadership is that no single theory or approach will work in all situations" (p. 18). The key leadership words here are "influence," "motivation," and "power," and no single approach will work in all situations. Rather, there are nine different ways or forms of power that can be used by a leader to motivate and influence others (Bulach, 1999).

In this chapter, the authors describe these nine distinctly different forms of power. The use and misuse of these forms of power are also described. Five are "freeing" forms of power. They give subordinates control without giving up control. They are intrinsic motivators, and they give leaders a systematic framework for adapting their leadership style to create a culture where subordinates are motivated to grow professionally. When these five forms of power are used, servant leadership is the style being used.

The other four forms of power are "controlling" forms. They are extrinsic motivators and restrict and control the actions of subordinates. When these four forms of power are used to meet the needs of the people and the organization, servant leadership is still the form of leadership being used. When they are used to meet the individual needs of the leader (self-serving), servant leadership is not in place.

A THEORY OF LEADERSHIP AND MOTIVATION

Many successful school leaders are embracing the concepts of total quality management, teamwork, and shared decision making as a way of empowering subordinates. Burns (1994) discussed this concept of empowerment and claimed that it is a "buzzword" and that often subordinates are not really empowered. He maintained that leaders should create conditions where subordinates are able to empower themselves. In other words, an organizational culture has to be created where "empowerment can come to life" (p. 48).

The problem of how to give control without giving up control and create conditions to empower subordinates is further exacerbated if the leader's style does not lend itself to shared decision making. Many leaders have a directive style with a high need to control. Leaders with this style tend to resort to position, reward, and coercion power to control subordinates.

Dilenschneider (1994) stated that when authority and power are practiced by directive, they will not continue to work. Further, he wrote that if power is the ability to get things done, it must be done through others. A key word here is the word "through" as opposed to the word "with." Directive leaders tend to get their work accomplished "with" the help of subordinates rather than "through" their help.

Debruyn (1986) maintained that the only way to keep power is to share it. He believes that many leaders abuse power, and in the end they lose it. The key is to share power and allow subordinates to have some control over the decision-making process. According to Bennis (1958), power is defined as control. He who controls has power, and if subordinates are given some control of the decision-making process, they are being empowered. Not only are they being empowered, but as Haskin (1995) stated, involving subordinates in the decision causes them to take more responsibility for the outcome of the decisions.

This increased responsibility tends to boost the power of the leader (Lammers, 1967). One such organizational plan for implementing a shared decision-making process and empowering subordinates was described by Bulach (1978). His plan required that all teachers, administrators, and support staff serve on one of 25 committees that met monthly to make decisions about curriculum and other district initiatives. These committees were responsible for revising a segment of the curriculum, and sometimes were asked to make recommendations to the superintendent on district-wide issues.

Some subordinates, however, are immature and do not want to be involved in the decision-making process. Hersey and Blanchard's (2012) theory of situational leadership requires that a leader consider the maturity or immaturity level of subordinates in selecting a style of leadership. A person with low motivation and little expertise is classified by Hersey and Blanchard as immature, and the appropriate leadership style is to be directive.

According to Hersey and Blanchard when subordinates become more motivated and experienced, a leader's style should be modified. For example, if subordinates are very immature, a directive style of leadership will work, and a collaborative or nondirective style will not. A servant leader has to be creative in moving them from a low-maturity level to a higher level. This can only be accomplished by giving them some control (empower) without giving up control.

Modifying a leader's style requires the use of differing forms of power. For example, position, reward, and coercion power, or the controlling forms of power, are normally used with immature subordinates, while the freeing forms of power may be all that are necessary with mature subordinates. These forms of power are used when the leadership style is collaborative or nondirective.

PURPOSE OF THIS CHAPTER

In this chapter, the authors describe a style of leadership where the five freeing and four controlling forms of power can be used to motivate and empower subordinates depending on their maturity level. Leaders must be able to influence and motivate subordinates both intrinsically and extrinsically. The nine forms of power are described and categorized according to the extent they are intrinsic or extrinsic motivators and foster dependence or independence. The use and misuse of these forms of power are also described.

As mentioned earlier, the key words used to describe leadership are "power," "influence," and "motivation." These words and other key terms described in this leadership theory are defined as follows:

- **power**: the ability to influence, control, and empower others.
- **influence**: the ability to motivate others.
- **motivation**: a process that causes others to sustain or change a behavior as a result of an extrinsic or intrinsic source.
- **leadership**: something that occurs when the leader motivates others (through use of the nine forms of power) to sustain or change a behavior.
- **dependence**: the subordinate is controlled (depowered) by the leader, and the motivation is extrinsic.
- **independence**: the subordinate is in control (empowered), and the motivation is intrinsic.
- **empowerment**: giving subordinates some control of the decision-making process and allowing them to be independent of the leader. *Note:* A leader who empowers does not give up control.
- **depowerment**: the subordinates do not have control of the decision-making process, and they are dependent on the leader.

Variations of the above definitions occur with the two different types of these nine forms of power. The two different types are: (1) those freeing forms that involve subordinates in the decision-making process and (2) those controlling forms that tell subordinates what to do. The five freeing forms of power foster independence of the leader, empower subordinates, and are intrinsic motivators. This occurs because subordinates have some control of the decision-making process. They are allowed to respond to a given situation and decide what to do. These forms of power are called freeing forms of power because subordinates are free to decide what will be done. They are given some control of the situation, but the leader has not given up control.

The four controlling forms of power foster dependence on the leader, depower subordinates, and are extrinsic motivators.. This occurs because subordinates are not in control of the decision-making process. These forms of power are called controlling forms of power because subordinates are told what to do (controlled) by the leader.

WHY ARE CARING BEHAVIORS AND CONTROL IMPORTANT FOR A HIGH-PERFORMING SCHOOL CULTURE?

We believe that there are two fundamental needs that determine human behavior, whether in a classroom, school, home, or community. Those two needs are the need to have some control over your life and existence and the need to feel/believe that others care about you. We are presenting a theory of life or human behavior here with which you may agree or disagree. In order to give some background on how we came up with this theory, we cite the work of Nietzsche (1910).

He examined other philosophies on why people behave the way they do. One such philosophy was that people behave the way they do because they want to be happy. Another philosophy at that time was that people behave the way they do because they want to be alive. They want to live and that's what motivates them to behave the way they do.

Nietzsche looked at these philosophies and disagreed. He theorized that there was a more essential need and that was the "will to power." He theorized that the need for power was more essential than life or happiness. We tend to agree with Nietzsche's theory, but we look at power as control. With power you gain control and what is life, if you do not have control. The feeling is one of hopelessness and it is not a good one! It is human nature to make every effort to maintain control of your life. Just look at human history and the wars that have been fought to gain control.

We can also look at US diplomacy and how we use our military and money to control what happens in other countries. This feeling of being controlled by the United States, in many instances, is resented and not appreciated. In chapter 1, we presented the high-performing school culture and how to give control to students without giving up control. However, we tend to disagree that human behavior is only about control.

There is another fundamental need and that is the knowledge and feeling that others care about you. This topic was covered in depth in chapter 2 where five sets of behaviors that create a caring learning environment were presented. They are:

• behaviors that reduce anxiety
• listening behaviors
• rewarding behaviors
• recognition behaviors
• friendship behaviors

According to the theory presented in chapter 2, if a student believes no one cares, learning will not take place. Instead unhappiness, poor attendance, dropouts, and even suicide are likely results. In this regard, the US diplomacy is on target. More than any other nation in the world we care about what happens in the rest of the world, but how about our classrooms and schools?

The organization called the Eunice Kennedy Shriver National Center for Community of Caring at "Communityofcaring.org" is a good resource on the importance of caring behaviors in a school. If you agree that being cared for and having control are important for an effective school culture, then you will find the nine forms of power great tools for helping to create a culture where these two essential needs can be met.

THE NINE FORMS OF POWER

French and Raven's (1959) original typology of power included five forms of power: (a) expertise, (b) referent, (c) position, (d) reward, and (e) coercion. These forms of power are included in the nine forms of power described in this chapter. We have added information, connection, moral, and ego power to the original typology of power. Information power was first described by Raven and Kruglanski (1975). Connection power was described by Hersey and Goldsmith (1980). Moral power was described by Sergiovanni, Starratt, and Cho (2013). Ego power is Bulach's contribution and is described later in this chapter. The nine forms of power help to create a culture where an individual's five basic needs can be met. These were described in chapter 1 (life, happiness, control, purpose, and caring).

FREEING FORMS OF POWER

There are five freeing forms of power: (1) information, (2) expertise, (3) personality, (4) ego, and (5) moral power. We call these freeing forms of power because they give control without giving up control. We use the word "empowerment" with the freeing forms because giving control to others is a form of empowerment.

The first form of power is information power. Dilenschneider (1994) maintained that knowledge is power. Knowledge is information, and it is used daily by the news media to influence their audience. According to Toffler (1990), knowledge or information is the most versatile form of power. He wrote that it requires the least amount of energy and provides "the biggest bang for the buck" (p. 16).

Information can be used by a leader to involve subordinates in the decision-making process and empower them. For example, if the leader wants subordinates to change the way they are doing something, the leader can explain the benefits of the change. Handouts, videos, or other information extolling the advantages of the change can also be made available. Subordinates, after analyzing the information, can make a decision. If subordinates decide to change, they are empowered, and the motivation for the change is intrinsic. The decision is made independent of the leader.

Expertise is the second form of power. The use of expertise also allows subordinates to choose a course of action. A leader who has expertise can demonstrate how to perform a task. Subordinates who watch the demonstration decide whether they are able to perform that task. Dilenschneider (1994) maintained that competence or expertise is the source of power and that leaders without competence cannot maintain power.

While Dilenschneider is correct, in today's complicated world, a leader cannot be an expert in all things. Consequently, leaders sometimes have to use the expertise of others to motivate subordinates to change. For example, if a new technique will benefit an organization, the leader can send key subordinates to another organization where that technique is being successfully utilized. The subordinates can observe the new process, and decide whether it is beneficial and if it will work in their organization. Subordinates who are exposed to this form of power frequently choose to imitate or adapt what they have observed. It is their choice, the motivation is intrinsic, they are independent of the person with the expertise, and they have been empowered.

It is easy to confuse information power with expertise power because a person who is an expert in his or her field usually has lots of information about that profession. Information power, as used here, however, always refers to some type of language, for example, written, verbal, video, and so forth. A teacher might implement integrated thematic instruction after reading a report on how it improves student achievement. Expertise power, however, occurs when someone physically demonstrates something or sees it happening. If the same teacher observed a teacher who was an expert on this type of instruction, that would be expertise power.

Information and expertise power are often combined. For example, when an expert shares information, it is more powerful and carries more weight than if the information came from a less reliable source. It is for this reason that experts tend to be used by advertisers when products are being promoted—for example, Michael Jordan's promotion of basketball shoes.

A leader, who has personality, or referent power, is described by Hersey and Blanchard (2012) as a person who is generally liked and admired by others because of personality and that is what allows them to motivate and influence others. When this form of power is used by a leader, it usually comes in the form of a request (verbal) or signal (nonverbal). The subordinate hears the request or sees the signal and changes behavior to comply with the leader's wishes. The change in behavior is done willingly and is intrinsically motivated, and the subordinate remains independent of the leader. The subordinate makes a conscious decision to grant the leader's wishes.

A form of power not previously mentioned in the literature is ego power. This form of power is used when the leader goes to a subordinate and says something like, "You did a beautiful job organizing that last project! Would you be willing to take responsibility for this one?" Another example might be, "If anybody here can handle this, I am confident you can!" When ego power is used, the subordinate's self-esteem and caring needs are filled, and the subordinate is willing to take on and is open to the new experience. The subordinate voluntarily chooses to follow the leader's wishes. The subordinate remains independent of the leader, the motivation is intrinsic, and the subordinate has been empowered.

Ego power can be used in its negative form as well. For example, the leader might say, "I don't know if this might be too difficult for you. What do you think?" Another example might be, "The people over at Plant B or School A are able to produce a better product than us. Are they better than we are?" The use of the negative ego stroke can be perceived by the subordinate as a challenge.

A real live example of this negative ego stroke is Muhammed Ali, who was quoted in a Bottom Line Personal pamphlet as saying that his teacher told him when he was 12 years old that he would never amount to anything. After winning the Golden Glove for boxing at the 1960 Rome Olympics, the first thing he did was go to that teacher and show her his medal and tell her that "he was the greatest."

This is a powerful leadership technique because subordinates who rise to this challenge tend to be very motivated. The subordinate sets out to prove to the leader, as did Mohammed Ali with his teacher, that he or she has the ability that has been challenged. Again, the subordinate remains independent of the leader, the motivation is intrinsic, and the subordinate has been empowered.

Moral power is the fifth and final freeing form of power that empowers subordinates. It allows them to remain independent and is an intrinsic motivator. Sergiovanni, Starratt, and Cho (2013) described moral power as the obligations and duties derived from widely shared values, ideas, and ideals.

Leaders who use this form of power have vision and mission statements that convey expectations and a handbook that contains rules and regulations. They also use the "expectations diagnosis" (in chapter 2) to arrive at a consensus regarding a set of expectations that describe what subordinates value and believe should occur in that organization. All who abide by these expectations can be said to be under the influence of moral power—that is, they abide by the values because it is the right thing to do. This form of power, once in place, requires the leader to do very little except to remind subordinates who are not living up to expectations of the right thing to do.

A servant leader who uses these freeing forms of power is involving subordinates in the decision-making process and creating conditions for them to grow. J. Martin Kohe (2004) stated that the greatest power that a person possesses is the power to choose.

When administrators and teachers use these forms of power, they are allowing choice and developing leadership capacity in subordinates. Lambert (2003) described the importance of developing leadership capacity for lasting school improvement. She described a high-performing school as an institution where "the principal shares power skillfully with teachers, parents, community members, and students" (p. 9). When administrators and teachers share power, they are giving control to others without giving up control, and that is a key component of the high-performing school culture. They also create a culture where the five basic needs of all individuals in the school environment are being met.

CONTROLLING FORMS OF POWER

The next four forms of power depower subordinates because subordinates are controlled by the leader, subordinates are dependent on the leader, and the motivation is extrinsic. They are (1) connection, (2) position, (3) reward, and (4) coercion power.

The first controlling form of power is connection power. Hersey and Goldsmith (1980) described this form of power as the perceived association a leader has with other influential people. If a subordinate perceives that a leader is well connected with superiors higher in the hierarchy, their power is enhanced. The subordinate knows that the leader has a greater ability to reward or punish than someone who is not so well connected. When this form of power is combined with position power, it gives the leader greater status and increases the likelihood that compliance/control will occur.

This form of power is different from all of the other forms of power. The other forms are gained because of something the leader does. This form is acquired through the eyes of the beholder. If they perceive that the leader has power, then the leader has power whether he or she has it or not. The motivation is extrinsic because the subordinate makes a decision to follow the leader based on the subordinate's perception that the leader's connections could result in some future benefit. The subordinate does what the leader asks or tells them to do because of a belief that the leader can follow through with a future reward or punishment as a result of compliance or noncompliance.

Position power refers to the authority and responsibility that have been assigned to a person holding an office. Position power is employed when the leader tells or orders a subordinate to do something. If a leader is liked, trusted, and respected by those superiors to whom the leader reports, position power is great. If the reverse is true, position power is weaker. When a leader uses his or her position to make a subordinate do something, the subordinate's motivation for doing things is extrinsic and the subordinate remains dependent on the leader.

Leaders who acquire position power also receive reward, coercion, and often connection power. Subordinates can either do what the leader directs them to do or suffer the consequences (coercion). Many leaders who rely on position power use rewards to motivate subordinates to do what they are told. When rewards fail to get the desired results, coercion or punishment is often used. If necessary, these types of leaders may use their connection power to increase their ability to reward and/or punish.

One interesting phenomenon is that position power depends a great deal on connection power. If subordinates perceive that the leader does not have connection power, then the leader's position power is weakened. For example, if subordinates know that the leader's contract has not been renewed, the leader's ability to use position power to tell subordinates what to do is greatly weakened.

In the final analysis, leaders who use the controlling forms of power rely on rewards and coercion as the major sources of motivation. This is not to say that these forms of power should not be used. For example, if a leader has very immature subordinates, the controlling forms of power are most effective. With position power there are obligations and responsibilities to meet organizational needs. When subordinates fail to meet organizational needs, position, reward, and coercion power must be used.

Lambert (2003) stated that leaders must deal with resistant teachers who refuse to participate in productive ways. The same holds true for teachers with their students. The controlling forms of power must be used with immature and resistant subordinates. The servant leader must serve both the needs of the organization and the needs of those subordinates who are more mature and motivated.

The error that many leaders make is using these controlling forms of power immediately without allowing subordinates to respond to one or more of the five freeing forms of power. One of the goals of servant leadership is creating situations where subordinates can make decisions independent of the leader. This empowers them and fulfills some of their needs, while at the same time meets the needs of the organization. Use of the five freeing forms of power also requires less effort than use of the four controlling forms of power. The ability to use the controlling forms of power can also be exhausted, where the freeing forms are almost inexhaustible.

The primary objective of school administrators and teachers is to give subordinates control within a highly controlled environment without giving up control.

OVERUSE OR MISUSE OF THE NINE FORMS OF POWER

Withholding information as a form of control over subordinates is not a good leadership technique. When information is withheld, subordinates are dependent on the leader for information and are kept in a subservient state. Subordinates in this type of organization tend to dislike the leader, and morale is low. Since the leader has the information, the subordinate remains dependent on the leader. Fiore (1999) found that leaders in organizations with negative cultures communicate with subordinates only when there are problems—that is, they withhold communication—while leaders in organizations with positive cultures are excellent communicators.

A second misuse is to provide too much information. The more information a leader shares with subordinates, the greater the chance that some information will be misinterpreted or that subordinates will experience an information overload. Determining the amount and kind of information to share with subordinates is a key leadership decision.

OVERUSE OR MISUSE OF EXPERTISE POWER

Demonstrating expertise too often or when it is not necessary can be viewed as being self-centered or "showing off." A leader must communicate altruistic tendencies (concern for others over concern for self) if trust is to develop. Subordinates have to believe that the leader cares about their welfare. Appearing self-centered or as a "show-off" is contrary to servant leadership. The secret to expertise power is to allow "others" to demonstrate their expertise and use theirs only when it is necessary.

OVERUSE OR MISUSE OF PERSONALITY POWER

Most leaders will readily admit that they frequently use this form of power to influence subordinates. However, leaders need to be cautioned because this form of power can be easily overused. For example, a leader can go to key personnel with requests too often and cause subordinates to grumble and make comments like "Here he or she comes again. I wonder what they want this time?"

OVERUSE OR MISUSE OF EGO POWER

Knowing who to stroke and when to stroke an ego is a judgment call. Negatively or positively stroking egos too often can be viewed as manipulative. If the positive ego stroke is used too often, subordinates might perceive that they are being used. Negatively stroking an ego can also garner the opposite result. For example, if the leader tells subordinates that a task might be too hard for them, they might agree that it is too hard. The negative ego stroke is one of the most powerful leadership techniques a leader can use. If done properly, the subordinate will overcome all obstacles to meet the challenge; however, it must be done with subordinates who have strong egos.

OVERUSE OR MISUSE OF MORAL POWER

Attempting to use moral power is a mistake when there is not an agreement on the expectations, values, and ideals that are to govern behavior. If agreement does not exist, the leader is imposing his or her set of values on the subordinates. This is contrary to the servant leadership concept. One of the first things a leader should do as the new head of an organization is foster a common understanding and agreement of the expectations that are going to be enforced and the values that are going to be rewarded. The process of arriving at this common understanding of values and beliefs is described in chapter 2 in the "expectations diagnosis."

OVERUSE OR MISUSE OF POSITION POWER

The overuse or misuse of position power can quickly extinguish its influence. Subordinates will rebel against the leader or undermine the leader's authority to the extent that organizational needs will no longer be met. The leader's superior(s) may transfer or fire a leader who cannot meet needs. The underuse of position power can lead to similar consequences. If a leader has position power, he or she must use it when subordinates and superiors expect it to be used, or they will lose it. Once subordinates determine that a leader is reluctant to use position power, they will begin challenging decisions, thereby weakening the leader's position power, until finally the leader loses his or her position in the organization.

OVERUSE OR MISUSE OF REWARD POWER

Failure to reward people when they are deserving can cause severe morale problems. Leaders who have favorite subordinates who receive greater rewards than those who are less favored are misusing reward power. Lunenburg and Ornstein (2012) described Porter and Lawler's (1968) "equity/expectancy theory" of motivation. The essence of the theory is that when some employees receive greater outcomes (rewards) for the same input, there is a lack of equity. Those who receive less reward for the same input will perceive it as a lack of equity or fairness and be less motivated. Another mistake is to overuse reward power to the point that the reward loses meaning. Overuse of this power can create a "what's in it for me" mentality, where subordinates will not work unless they know they will be rewarded.

Regarding rewards as a source of motivation, Sergiovanni, Starratt, and Cho (2013) stated that there are three ways to motivate subordinates:

- "what gets rewarded gets done" approach
- "what is rewarding gets done" approach
- "what is good gets done" approach

The primary objective of reward power should be to move subordinates from what gets rewarded to what is rewarding and good. What gets rewarded is an extrinsic motivator, and what is rewarding and good are intrinsic motivators; however, this form of power is the one controlling form of power that can be used by a leader for all subordinates regardless of their level of maturity. Even mature subordinates enjoy rewards. Consequently, leaders should not think of this as a form of power to use only with immature subordinates. One objective of leadership is the judicious use of reward power along with the five freeing forms of power.

OVERUSE OR MISUSE OF COERCION POWER

Leaders who quickly resort to coercion as a way to induce subordinate compliance will soon lose their position because their leaderships will be met with resistance. Bullying behavior is one other misuse of coercion power that often occurs. There are bullies in many organizations who coerce their colleagues. *The Atlanta Journal-Constitution* featured an article on bullying behavior that stated, "Bullying—one of the most insidious and fastest-growing forms of workplace violence—is on the rise worldwide" (Joyner, 1999, Section R-1, p. 1).

Leaders must act to curb bullies who are coercing their colleagues. Bullying behavior has become particularly prevalent in the school setting. Brazelton (2014) writes about bullying behavior in a number of settings. She describes teenage meanness, bullying behavior, and the devastating consequences. Bulach (2012), in an article for a parent magazine, described what can be done to reduce bullying behavior. He suggests that leaders who overuse controlling forms of power exacerbate the problem while leaders who use the freeing forms reduce the problem. A bully, he writes, has a high need to control, and bullying is the way to get that need met. Leaders must become more cognizant of bullying behavior and find ways to control it.

OVERUSE OR MISUSE OF CONNECTION POWER

Misuse of connection power is often associated with the use of threats regarding what to do if a subordinate does not comply with a request or demand. For example, "I am going to tell the boss if you don't get to work!" Use of power in this way implies that a leader is relying on their connection power and not their positon power. The failure to use their position power always weakens their own power. According to Cohen (2002), when position power is not used, their ability to be the leader is always weakened.

Another misuse of connection power is the leader who tries to create the illusion of this form of power by name dropping. Leaders who drop names are trying to create the illusion that they are connected. This practice tends to decrease the leader's power because subordinates often see through this ruse.

CONCLUSION

The five freeing forms of power—information, expertise, personality, ego, and moral power—can be used to motivate subordinates by empowering them. They also give control without giving up control. When used properly, the servant leader can use them to help move subordinates from one level of maturity to higher levels of maturity. When these forms of power are used, the subordinate decides the course of action. If they decide to follow their leader, the form of motivation is intrinsic because they see that course of action as a good thing to do. Further, they are allowed the independence of choice, and they are empowered in the process. As subordinates become more mature, the leadership style can become more collaborative and less directive.

The four controlling forms of power—connection, position, reward, and coercion power—should be used with immature subordinates, and only when the five freeing forms of power do not work. The controlling forms of power must be used by the servant leader if the freeing forms of power are not motivating subordinates and when subordinates are not meeting organizational needs. Keep in mind that the judicious use of reward power, while not a freeing form of power, nevertheless, is a good form of power.

When the controlling forms of power are used, subordinates must comply or face the displeasure/position power of the leader and forgo the reward or receive a punishment/coercion. Subordinates have no choice, are in a dependent position, and are being controlled by the leader. Connection power enhances a leader's position power and increases his or her ability to reward or punish.

Who has the most power is an interesting question. A leader who has position power and connection power will be very powerful only if they use the five freeing forms of power. All leaders have the ability to use all nine forms of power. Those leaders who use all nine will be very powerful. Those that use only the controlling forms and occasionally some of the freeing forms will be less powerful.

The goal of servant leadership should be to move away from the old forms of bureaucracy that rely on position, reward, and coercion power toward a high-performing culture that relies on information, expertise, personality, ego, and moral power. A bureaucracy fosters dependency and relies on extrinsic motivation, whereas a high-performing school empowers faculty and students and relies on intrinsic motivation. In a bureaucracy, leaders control subordinates to make sure they do "things right" (position power), as opposed to a high-performing culture where the focus is on doing the "right thing" (moral power).

The objective for leaders is to create an organizational culture where subordinates are actively involved in the decision-making process. In order for this to happen, the leader, according to Abrashof (2012), has to be less controlling and give control without giving up control. Control is one of the five basic needs that determine human behavior. The five freeing forms of power are leadership techniques that allow this to be accomplished.

The word "freeing" is used because the subordinate has control and is independent and "free" to make their own decision. They have the power and are in control. When subordinates do not do the right thing, the controlling forms of power must be used to make them comply. The word "controlling" is used because the subordinate is dependent and does not have "control" of the decision.

Knowing when and how to free subordinates and give them control (empower) and when to take control (depower) is the sine qua non of effective leadership and being able to motivate subordinates. While this chapter describes the role of the servant leader with subordinates, the reader needs to keep in mind that the same principles apply to a teacher as the servant leader for students in a classroom.

Whether as a teacher, principal, parent, or any other role, a servant leader gives control without giving it up, empowers others, helps others, shares leadership, creates independence, builds trust, and creates a caring learning environment in which everyone is focused on how to improve conditions for others. We believe that there are basic needs that determine human behavior, whether in a classroom, school, or anywhere. These basic needs are life, happiness, control, purpose, and caring. These needs can only be met if leaders use all nine forms of power.

Note: When the words "leaders" and "subordinates" are used, the words "administrators and/or faculty" and "students" can be substituted.

REFERENCES

Abrashoff, M. D. (2012). *It's your ship: Management techniques from the best damn ship in the navy.* (10th ed.). Tempe, AZ: Warner Business.

Bazelon, E. (2014). *Sticks and stones: Defeating the culture of bullying and rediscovering the power of character and empathy.* Manhattan, NY: Random House.

Bennis, W. G. (1958). *Authority, power, and the ability to influence.* Human Relations. 11(2). 143–155.

Bulach, C. R. (1978). *An organizational plan for curriculum development.* Educational Leadership. 35(4). 308–314.

Bulach, C. R. (1999, November). *Motivating subordinates: Nine leadership techniques.* A presentation at the Southern Regional Council of Education Administration. Charleston, North Carolina.

Bulach, C. R. (2012, Fall). *What you can do about bullying behavior.* Woodbury Magazine.

Burns, G. (1994). *The trouble with empowerment.* Quality Digest. 14(2). 47–49.

Cohen, A. H. (2002). *Why life sucks and what you can do about it.* San Diego, CA: Jodere Group.

Debruyn, R. L. (1986). *The only way to keep power.* The Master Teacher. 18(6). 1–2.

Dilenschneider, R. L. (1994). *On power.* New York: HarperCollins.

Fiore, D. J. (1999). *The relationship between principal effectiveness and school culture in elementary schools.* Unpublished doctoral dissertation, Indiana State University, Terre Haute, Indiana.

French, J. R. P., & Raven, B. (1959). "The bases of social power." In D. Cartwright (Ed.). *Studies in social power* (pp. 150–167). Ann Arbor: University of Michigan. Institute for Social Research.

Haskin, K. (1995, April). *A process of learning: The principal's role in participatory management.* Paper presented at the annual meeting of the American Educational Research Association. San Francisco, California.

Hersey, P., & Blanchard, K. (2012). *Management of organizational behavior.* Englewood Cliffs, NJ: Prentice Hall (10th ed.).

Hersey P., & Goldsmith, M. (1980, April). *The changing role of performance management.* Training and Development Journal. 34(10). 18.

Joyner, T.(1999, August 29). "Bullies on the rise." *Atlanta Journal-Constitution.* Section R-1. p. 1.

Kohe, J. M. (2004). *Your greatest power.* Wise, VA: The Napoleon Hill Foundation.

Lambert, L. (2003). *Leadership capacity for lasting school improvement.* Alexandria, VA: Association for Supervision and Curriculum Development.

Lammers, C. J. (1967). *Power and participation in decision-making in formal organizations.* American Journal of Sociology. 73(9). 201–216.

Lunenburg, F. C., & Ornstein, A. C. (2012). *Educational administration*. Belmont, CA: Wadsworth Publishing Company (6th ed.).

McDowelle, J. O., & Buckner, K. (2002). *Leading with emotion: Reaching balance in educational decision-making*. Lanham, MD: Scarecrow Press.

Nietzsche, F. (1910). "The will to power. An attempted transvaluation of all values. Books one and two." In Oscar Levy. *The complete works of Friedrich Nietzsche*. 14. Edinburgh and London: T.N. Foulis. Retrieved on 7-25-1015 from http://www.archive.org/details/completeworksrie033168mbp. (Revised third edition 1925, published by The Macmillan Company).

Porter, L. W., & Lawler, E. E. (1968). *Managerial attitudes and performance*. Homewood, IL: Irwin Press.

Raven, B. H., & Kruglanski, W. (1975). "Conflict and power." In P. G. Swingle (Ed.). *The structure of conflict* (pp. 177–219). New York: Academic Press.

Sergiovanni, T., Starratt, R., & Cho V. (2013). *Supervision: A redefinition* (9th ed.). New York: McGraw-Hill.

Toffler, A. (1990). *Powershift*. New York: Bantam Books.

Chapter 5

A Character Education Program That Is the Foundation of a High-Performing School (Phase IV)

In chapter 1 (Phase I), we described the four types of school cultures and provided data on how the high-performing school culture improves time on task, improves school culture and climate, and eventually improves test scores. A process for continuing to reshape the culture of a school was described in chapters 2 and 3 (Phase II). In chapter 4, the use and misuse of the nine forms of power and their impact on a school's culture and climate were described (Phase III).

According to Walsh (2004) and Berger (2003), the entire school community must be involved in order to create a high-performing school. Berger stated: "Though society debates the question of whether schools should teach values, the process of schooling itself imbues values—we have no choice about this. If we want citizens who value integrity, respect, responsibility, compassion, and hard work, we need to build school cultures that model those attributes" (p. 7).

Sipos (2014) agreed by citing David Brooks, a New York columnist, who stated that character education works best when it is intentional and permeates the entire school culture and curriculum. In this chapter we will describe a character education program that involves everyone and permeates the curriculum. We will also describe how "social contracting" can play a role in a character education program and a high-performing school.

WHAT IS A CHARACTER EDUCATION PROGRAM?

A character education program is any effort to shape student, faculty, and community behavior related to selected character traits. According to Bulach

(2002), a character trait is something that affects a person's relationship with others. However, he also said that there is a self-component for some character traits, for example, persistence or responsibility. Consequently, he defined a character trait as an intrinsic attitude or belief that determines a person's behavior in relation to "**other people**" and in relation to "**self.**" Further, he stated that all character traits fall into one of these two groups: those that determine how we behave with others and those that determine our self-behavior.

Such character traits as sportsmanship, generosity, kindness, respect for others, courtesy, and empathy have behaviors that are easily observable in relation to **other people**. Character traits such as persistence, responsibility, honesty, self-respect, and self-control have behaviors that relate more to **self** and are not easily observable. Consequently, there are two types of character traits: those that relate to **self** and those that relate to **others**.

Many schools in the United States have mandated character education programs, but according to Prestwich (2004), there is little agreement on how teachers and school officials should approach this task. Bulach (2003a) found school officials using a variety of different curriculums for their character education programs. Some schools have purchased canned curriculums, and others have developed their own. Some have set aside a certain time of the week to deliver the character education curriculum or have delivered it while a certain subject is being taught, and others have infused it throughout the day. Some schools focus on a character trait of the week and others focus on a character trait of the month.

Bulach (2003a) recommended that schools align their curriculum so that traits that relate to **others** are the focus in one semester and traits that relate to **self** are the focus the next semester. He stated that mixing the two does not allow for curriculum scope and sequence. For example, respect for others, courtesy, kindness, and compassion all have similar behaviors that relate to others. Conversely, persistence, responsibility, accountability, dependability, honesty, and self-respect have similar behaviors that relate to self. When grouped by type, teaching one trait is reinforced by the others.

WHY IS A CHARACTER EDUCATION PROGRAM IMPORTANT IN A HIGH-PERFORMING SCHOOL?

In 25 schools in Georgia, Bulach (2003b) found a correlation of +0.71 ($p < 0.001$) between the culture and climate of a school and student behavior related to 16 sets of character traits. In 193 schools in West Virginia, he found a significant positive relationship of +0.34 ($p < 0.00$) between achievement and character scores.

Since there is a significant statistical relationship between culture and climate, character behavior, and student achievement, it makes sense to include a character education program as an integral part of a high-performing school. This character program, if it is to be successful, must involve the entire school community: faculty, students, parents, and all other citizens. Implementation of this character education program is Phase IV of the plan for a high-performing school.

IMPLEMENTING A CHARACTER EDUCATION PROGRAM

Current character education programs focus on a character trait of the week or month and tend to be cognitive in orientation. This creates three problems: **First**, the focus tends to be on knowledge of the trait rather than on the behaviors associated with the trait. This creates a situation where students may know more about a trait, but the behaviors associated with that trait have not changed. The student also receives mixed messages about a trait because faculty members have different interpretations of it.

The **second** problem is the level of commitment of the faculty. Some faculty members do not participate in the character education program. Additionally, after two or three years of doing the same trait of the week, boredom with the process begins to take place. Bulach (2003b) found that a number of schools, particularly at the middle- and high-school levels, had lower scores in year four of the grant than in year one. In questioning faculty and students about this decline, they stated that it was the same thing every year, and a lot of teachers had stopped doing it.

The **third** problem is the character education curriculum. Most state mandates require school officials to implement a character education curriculum. Typically, the character education curriculum focuses on a different character trait for the week or month. This change in focus on the next character trait makes it difficult to involve parents and the community. Involving parents and the community is essential for an effective character education program. If the character education program is to be successful, it must address these three limitations of current character education programs.

If parents and the community are to be involved, a school and/or school district should focus on a character trait for the year or semester. School officials do not have to change their current character education program. Many are required by law to teach all character traits each year. However, they can focus on one trait per semester or year along with their current program. A great trait to start such a program is "respect for others" or "courtesy."

Littky and Grabelle (2004) maintained that respect for others or courtesy must be present in order to build and cultivate a positive school culture. They stated, "We must have and demonstrate respect for others, for ourselves, and for the building itself. If kids are going to be respectful, they must feel respected" (p. 55). Correlations on the 16 sets of character traits in the four-year Georgia study ranged from a high of +0.97 to a low of +0.80. Consequently, if behaviors associated with "courtesy" are improved, a corresponding improvement in behaviors associated with all other character traits will also occur. A survey that measures these 16 sets of character traits has been developed. See Appendix E to see the 16 sets of character traits. A report, graph, and cover letter generated by this survey can be found at http://www.westga.edu/~cbulach/.

IDENTIFYING THE BEHAVIORS ASSOCIATED WITH A TRAIT

It is important to identify the behaviors associated with a trait. It may have one meaning for a student from the projects, one meaning for a minority student, one meaning for a cook, one meaning for a bus driver, one meaning for a parent, and another meaning for people at a school in North Dakota versus one in Florida. How can school officials identify the behaviors associated with a trait for their school? The process is surprisingly simple as follows: (again there is no magic in three 3 × 5 cards—use more or less as appropriate for your setting):

- The teacher should give students three 3 × 5 index cards and tell them that the focus of the semester (or year) will be on "courtesy." They should ask them what they would want people at the school to do or say to them to show them "courtesy." The teacher should then instruct them to write one behavior on each card. Tell them they can't write "yes sir," "no sir," or "thank you," as these will occur on most cards.
- The teacher should collect all the cards and sort them into piles of common behaviors, and paraphrase those where there is agreement that a behavior is indicative of "courtesy."
- Faculty members should also be given 3 × 5 index cards with the same instructions.
- At some event where a number of parents are present, they should be given cards with the same instructions.
- Business partners should be given cards with the same instructions.
- All returned cards should be given to a committee or coordinator who identifies about 10 behaviors indicative of "courtesy" at that school.
- A chart of these behaviors should be made for each classroom, hallway, the cafeteria, and so forth. This chart should also be sent home for parents to place on their refrigerator or elsewhere.

- The same chart should be sent to all business partners. If this is a district initiative as opposed to a school initiative, the chamber of commerce can be asked to make a copy of the chart for their members.

When the chart goes up at the school, at home, and at community businesses, everyone is likely to recognize a behavior they have written. Since everyone has been part of the process and recognizes their contribution, they are more likely to buy in and support the character education program. The identified behaviors can now be made a part of the high-performing school disciplinary program. The desired behaviors associated with the selected trait can be reinforced when they are seen, and when those behaviors have not been demonstrated, they can be extinguished through the use of redirects. Below are some behaviors that were identified when I used this process:

- Don't interrupt when others are talking.
- Don't use curse words or "bad language."
- Don't call each other names.
- Say things, like, "Thank you," "Pardon me."
- Listen when someone talks to you.
- Don't ignore others.
- Don't talk back to teachers and other adults.

The concept of servant leadership is also reinforced through the focus on "courtesy." When everyone is focused on showing courtesy to others, a fundamental change occurs in the school setting. Normally students, and to some extent faculty, tend come across as self-serving. In related research, Bulach, Fullbright, and Williams (2003) found that 50% of students had a negative response on the behavior "people care about each other at our school." A focus on "courtesy" should decrease self-serving behaviors and increase serving others and caring behaviors. Everyone, including students, becomes a servant leader.

The above process requires no curriculum or time set aside to implement. Everyone, including cafeteria workers, custodians, bus drivers, and secretaries, can be involved in the process of reinforcing desirable behavior and extinguishing undesirable behavior. Parents and the community are also encouraged to participate in the character education program.

The old adage that it takes a community to raise a child is more likely to occur if parents are involved. According to Berger (2003), the culture that is created in a school has to be shared by parents and the community. He also believes that this shared culture impacts student achievement. Focusing on one character trait for a year or semester allows this shared culture to develop.

This process encourages reinforcement when a behavior associated with the trait occurs and legitimizes an intervention when behavior is inappropriate. It also heightens parent and community awareness of the behaviors associated with a character trait. In many instances, parents and the community have never really considered what "courtesy" looks like in the home and community. Also, in many schools, character education occurs during a set time during the week or day, and it is not emphasized the entire day. The end result is an emphasis on improving behaviors associated with this trait during the entire six- to seven-hour school day, as well as the rest of the day in the home or community.

The character education curriculum focused on one trait each year or semester is essential to create a feeling of community in the school and each classroom. This feeling of community, according to Berger (2003), is essential for an effective school. Students feel safe in this type of school culture. They do not fear being bullied. They do not fear the risk of failure. They feel supported at the school, at home, and in the community. Everyone is focused on behaviors associated with one character trait.

The process can be repeated each semester or year for additional character traits. The next character trait that is recommended for focus is "responsibility." This trait determines behaviors related to self, while the previous one determines behaviors toward others. Of all the traits, it has the highest correlation with student achievement ($+0.41$, $p < 0.01$). The next semester or year should be followed with a trait related to behavior toward others and followed by one related toward self.

Another good trait to follow "courtesy" is "respect for others," or if bullying behavior is a problem, "compassion" might be selected. A good trait to follow "responsibility" is "self-respect." This reinforces the efforts of the Safe and Drug Free federal mandate and helps reduce alcohol and drug abuse as well as sexual promiscuity. It also addresses the major school problem of cursing.

The Bulach (2003b) research, in both Georgia and West Virginia, found that using foul language or cursing always receives the most negative scores. While we have stated that you can focus on one trait each semester, we recommend focusing on one trait each year. That way everyone is focused and committed and each year the focus is on a different trait. The current problem of boredom with most character education programs can be eliminated.

THE ROLE OF SOCIAL CONTRACTING

Social contracting has been discussed and written about for centuries and goes back to Jean Jacques Rosseau (1800). More information on social contracting can be found at http://www.fordham.edu/halsall/mod/Rousseau-soccon.html. On page one of this site, we find these words:

> At a point in the state of nature when the obstacles to human preservation have become greater than each individual with his own strength can cope with . . . , an adequate combination of forces must be the result of men coming together. Still, each man's power and freedom are his main means of self-preservation. How is he to put them under the control of others without damaging himself . . . ?

A well-designed character education program is focused on how people come together or treat each other and how they treat themselves (self-preservation). It is also true that there are many obstacles to having a high-performing school culture. That is why it would be very helpful if each student had some form of social contract regarding how they were going to behave in that school setting. The same could be said for all the faculties at the school, but we are only going to focus on a social contract for students. We want the students to come together and agree on a set of behaviors that will guide student behavior in that school.

We need to give students some control over the process of social contracting. In order to meet Rosseau's intent of "each man's power and freedom are his means of self-preservation," we need to give control without giving up control. Consequently, we advise letting students choose, from a set of behaviors, the ones they wish to govern their behavior. How this set of behaviors is developed is left to the faculty of each school. The behaviors at a rural school in Indiana could be quite different from those at a school in Atlanta, Georgia. Some examples of behaviors a student could choose from include the following:

• To do my homework.
• To stop using cuss words.
• To help a student who is being picked on or bullied.
• To show respect and courtesy to others.
• To treat others the way I want to be treated.
• To tell the truth.
• To avoid the use of tobacco, alcohol, and drugs.
• To pay attention in class.
• To help others who are having a problem.
• To do what teachers ask us to do.

The lead sentence for these behaviors should be "I will do my best" and then have the student select from the list of behaviors generated by the faculty at that school. By having students select the behaviors they agree to do their best to follow, you give the student control without giving up control. Since the students choose the behaviors they agree to follow, they are more likely to try and adhere to the contract they sign.

How many behaviors they choose from the ones identified by the faculty is up to each school's faculty. They could choose 7–10 or less. Each faculty should make the decision on how many behaviors will be in the contract. The important thing is to let students choose the behaviors. If they are forced to choose all of them, then you have not given control, and the conditions of social contracting would have been violated. Also putting "do my best," in the contract, gives them more control because it gives an escape when they are unable to comply with that behavior. When and where this contract is developed and signed is up to each school's administration and faculty. Certainly, it should be as each new student is enrolled and in front of his/her parents or guardian. Whether the parent or guardian also signs the contract should be a faculty decision. We think it would be a good decision to have the parent or guardian also sign.

There is another reason for a social contract. If you recall, we wrote that students needed to have some control over what happens to them, and they also needed to feel that caring behaviors were present. We also wrote that various philosophers stated that people behaved the way they do because they wanted to be happy and alive. We also believe that there is a fifth reason why people behave the way they do. People, or, in this case students, who have a purpose will behave differently than students who do not have a purpose.

Having students develop and sign a social contract gives them a purpose. Dr. Mehmet Oz and Rick Warren are both strong proponents of a purpose-driven life. If students are alive, are happy, have control, are cared for, and have a purpose, the five needs for why people behave the way they do are being met. The end result will be a school culture and climate for the creation of a high-performing school.

CONCLUSION

The overall impact of counting redirects, servant leadership, giving control without giving up control, the freeing forms of power versus controlling ones, the character education program, and social contract create a learning environment for a high-performing school. To use an analogy, think of baking a cake. Chapters 1–4 are mixing the ingredients and baking a cake.

The authors provide the recipe/elements that must come together to create the ideal environment for a positive culture and climate. In chapter 5, the character education program and social contract can be compared to icing the cake. This is the final touch that brings everything together for the entire school community.

The end result is a combination of processes that go together in a seamless fashion. Each can stand alone, yet each supports and reinforces the other. In chapter 1, we gave the six reasons for low test scores: poor school culture and climate, time lost to discipline, failure to meet basic needs, the wrong use of power to control, failure to involve parents and community, and poor levels of openness and trust. All six reasons are addressed in chapters 1–5. If the mission is to create a high-performing school where test scores are improved and dropouts and bullying are reduced, then this is a recipe or vision for accomplishing that mission.

FOUR HYPOTHESES

If teachers have more time to teach, and if the time students are on task increases, it is logical that test scores should increase. We do know that 30 graduate students implemented a "high-performing classroom" where there were fewer discipline problems, teachers had more time to teach, and the percentage of time students were on task did increase. We also know that four schools in Indiana implemented it on a school-wide basis and that student time on task increased about 75% (described in chapter 1).

We also know that there is a significant positive relationship between a school's culture, student achievement, dropout rate, and character behavior. Consequently, it is hypothesized that:

- school culture and climate will improve;
- any school that implements this reform will find an improvement in student achievement;
- there will be a greatly reduced dropout rate because students will enjoy attending this kind of school; and
- bullying behavior will be reduced.

Students will feel empowered and have a sense of control instead of being controlled. They will feel like someone cares about them. They will be motivated both intrinsically and extrinsically (described in chapter 4). They will have a sense of purpose and belonging. Finally, parents and community will feel an association with the school and will reinforce student behavior related to 16 sets of character traits (described in chapter 5).

Implementation of the school reform we have described in this book will meet with some resistance because it involves a change in the way things used to be. If further assistance is wanted, we have written a second book with many strategies for enhancing the reform that has been described in this book. The title of that book is *Enhancing a School's Culture and Climate: New Insights for Improving Schools.*

REFERENCES

Berger, R. (2003). *An ethic of excellence: Building a culture of craftsmanship with students.* Portsmouth, NH: Heineman.

Bulach, C. R. (2002). *Implementing a character education program and assessing its impact on student behavior.* The Clearinghouse. 76(2). 79–83.

Bulach, C. R. (2003a, November 16). *A four-year character education grant: What have we learned?* Presentation at the International Civic Education Conference. New Orleans, Louisiana.

Bulach, C. R. (2003b). *West Virginia character trait report. Research report detailing the results of the status of character education in all 55 school districts in West Virginia.* Presentation to the WV State Legislature.

Bulach, C. R., Fullbright P. J., & Williams, R. (2003). *Bullying behavior: What is the potential for violence at your school?* Journal of Instructional Psychology. 30(2). 156–164.

Jean Jacques Rousseau. (1800). *Contrat social ou Principes du droit politique* (Paris: Garnier Frères), pp. 240–332, passim. Translated by Henry A. Myers.

Littky, D., & Grabelle, S. (2004). *The big picture: Education is everybody's business.* Alexandria, VA: Association for Supervision and Curriculum Development.

Prestwich, D. L. (2004). *Character education in America's schools.* The School Community Journal. 14(1). 139–150.

Sipos, B. (2014, September). *Character matters.* Character Education Partnership. Retrieved 8-10-2015 from. http://character.org/articles/character-matters/.

Walsh, J. A. (2004). *Leadership for high-performance learning.* The LINK: A Publication for Education Practitioners. 22(2). 1–3.

Appendix A

Supervisory Climate Behaviors

Anyone wishing a copy of either survey should contact cbulach@comcast.net. There is no charge for use of the survey.

SUPERVISORY CLIMATE BEHAVIORS

Human Relations

My principal demonstrates a caring attitude.
My principal provides positive reinforcement.
My principal interacts with staff.
My principal remains distant.
My principal calls me by name.
My principal compliments me.
My principal does not listen.
My principal uses eye contact.
My principal models good communication skills.
My principal has not supported me when parents were involved.
My principal remembers what it is like to be a teacher.
My principal tells teachers to make do with what they have.
My principal involves me in decisions.

Trust/decision-making

My principal displays a lack of trust.
My principal uses coercion to motivate me.
My principal corrects me in front of others instead of privately.
My principal gossips about other teachers and/or administrators.

My principal "nit picks" on evaluations.
My principal makes "snap judgments."
My principal listens to both sides of the story before making a decision.
My principal implements the latest fads without thorough knowledge.
My principal bases evaluations on a short observation.
My principal evaluates situations carefully before taking action.
My principal makes decisions as "knee jerk" reactions to an incident.

Instructional Leadership
My principal provides feedback regarding my teaching.
My principal demonstrates a lack of vision.
My principal is knowledgeable about the curriculum.
My principal is knowledgeable about instructional strategies.
My principal shrugs off or devalues a problem or concern.
My principal frequently interrupts my teaching.
My principal applies procedures consistently.
My principal holds people accountable.
My principal fails to follow up.
My principal has rules, but does not always enforce them.

Conflict
My principal is able to keep a confidence.
My principal shows favoritism to some teachers.
My principal has double standards
My principal is partial to influential parents.
My principal supports me as a person even if I am wrong.
My principal is afraid to question his/her superiors.
My principal "passes the buck" rather than deal with the situation.

Control
My principal delegates responsibility.
My principal assigns too much paperwork.
My principal assigns duty during planning periods.
My principal expects work to be done "yesterday" with no notice.
My principal overemphasizes control.
My principal uses the words "I" and "my" too frequently.
My principal is rigid and inflexible.
My principal has rules, but does not always enforce them.

Note: All negative behaviors are underlined.

Appendix B

A Report of Caring Behaviors

(The mean scores are those of an elementary school)

CARING BEHAVIORS BY FACTOR

Mean Scores	Item #	Anxiety Factor
2.90	5	My teacher greets students when they enter my room.
4.72	6	My teacher calls students by their name.
2.73	7	My teacher gives students positive reinforcement for good behavior.
4.44	8	My teacher enforces the same rules for all students.
4.31	14	My teacher provides an orderly classroom.
4.43	17	My teacher creates an environment where students feel safe.
3.98	18	My teacher teaches students at their ability level.
4.37	20	My teacher maintains eye contact with students when I talk to him/her.
4.24	23	My teacher gives students cues when they don't understand or respond.
4.24	26	My teacher is positive with students.

		Listening Factor
2.08	15	My teacher takes a personal interest in what I do outside my classroom.
2.94	16	My teacher gives students opportunities to make decisions that affect them.

2.25	19	My teacher makes time for students before and after school.
3.18	21	My teacher asks students for their opinions.

Reward Factor

2.52	9	My teacher informs parents about their student's progress.
2.03	12	My teacher displays students' work.
1.84	25	My teacher asks students to help with classroom tasks.
2.44	27	My teacher provides students with "treats" and "goodies" on special occasions.

Friendship Factor

1.11	13	My teacher eats lunch with students.
3.46	22	My teacher returns work promptly with comments.
2.65	28	My teacher allows me to have fun at his/her expense.
3.49	30	My teacher intervenes when students pick on each other.

Predictability Factor

2.83	10	My teacher recognizes students for academic achievement.
2.24	11	My teacher recognizes students for extracurricular achievement.
4.48	24	My teacher uses negative criticism with students.
3.18	29	My teacher uses sarcasm with me.

Note: The mean score is a Likert scale and scores above 3.0 are positive and scores below are negative.

Appendix C

School Climate Graph

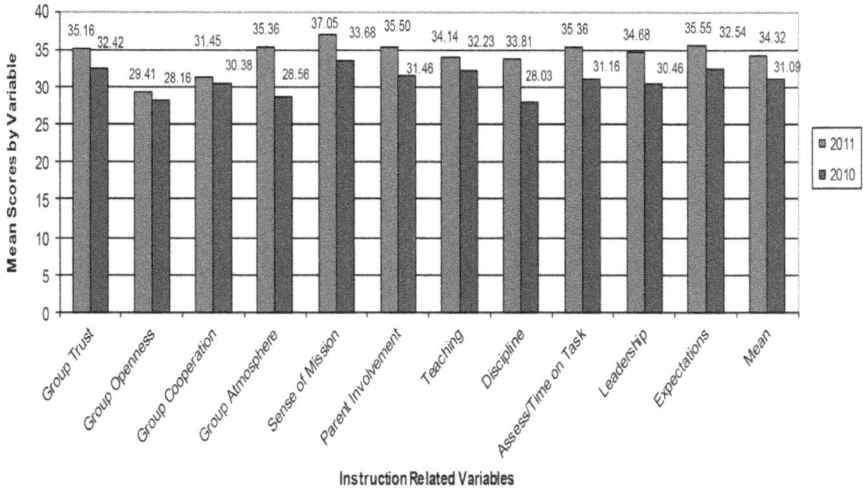

Appendix D

Instructional Improvement Survey

A Pre-2010 and Post-2011 Comparison of Measure of School Culture and Climate

The measure of school culture has four variables: (1) group openness, (2) group trust, (3) group cooperation, and (4) group atmosphere. The measure of school climate has seven variables: (1) sense of mission, (2) instructional leadership, (3) student discipline, (4) parent involvement, (5) assessment/time on task, (6) teaching practices, and (7) expectations. All items in italics are negative and must be reverse scored.

Definitions of each variable and the items that they measure are:

Group Trust: An interpersonal condition that exists when interpersonal relationships are characterized by an assured reliance or confident dependence on the character, ability, predictability, confidentiality, and truthfulness of others in the group.

Item # Mean Scores

	2011	2010	
15	3.90	3.62	Question others' intentions and/or motives.
16	3.23	3.30	Conceal your true feelings to what others do and/or say.
17	4.23	4.03	Count on others for assistance.
18	4.59	4.05	Believe that others care about you.
19	4.45	3.76	Deal with them directly when there is a problem.
20	4.68	3.95	Expect that they will respond favorably in a situation where your welfare is at stake.
21	4.59	4.14	Rely on them to keep a confidence.
22	4.50	4.16	Believe they are honest.

23	4.59	4.49	Count on them to do what they say they are going to do.
24	4.68	4.43	Tell the truth when it needs to be told.
25	4.77	4.51	Respect the opinions of your colleagues.
26	4.68	4.38	Admit mistakes and/or problems when necessary.
27	4.41	4.19	Support their ideas, decisions, and actions.
28	4.23	3.73	Behave consistently regardless of the person, situation, or level of stress.

Group Openness: An interpersonal condition that exists between people when (1) facts, ideas, values, beliefs, and feelings are shared and (2) the recipient of a transmission is willing to listen.

5	3.32	3.49	Tell others what you think of the way they do things.
6	3.59	3.49	Tell others what you think of their ideas, values, and beliefs.
7	3.91	3.76	Express your feelings.
8	3.82	3.27	Ask others what they think about the way you do things.
9	3.68	3.00	Ask others what they think about your ideas, values, and beliefs.
10	4.05	3.62	Ask others about their feelings.
11	4.00	4.19	Accept others' comments and reactions.
12	3.23	3.43	Disagree with others if you don't agree with what is being said or done.
13	4.00	3.76	Share positive thoughts with others instead of keeping them to yourself.
14	3.18	3.16	Share constructive criticism with others instead of keeping it to yourself.

Group Cooperation: An interpersonal condition that exists between the various constituents (teachers, staff, students, parents, and community) in the school setting.

48	4.18	3.70	Teachers are involved in the decision-making process.
49	4.23	3.76	A school leadership team or advisory council assists the administration with decisions.
50	1.95	3.81	A student leadership team or advisory council assists the administration with decisions.
51	3.91	3.86	A parent leadership team or advisory council assists the administration with decisions.

56	4.18	3.54	The administration keeps the constituents in the school setting adequately informed.
57	4.41	3.97	The constituents in the school setting are encouraged to communicate with the administration.
63	4.32	3.81	The degree of cooperation between the faculty and the administration is appropriate.
64	4.27	3.92	The degree of cooperation between the faculty and the staff is appropriate.

Group Atmosphere: A supportive interpersonal condition that exists between the constituents (teachers, staff, students, parents, and community) in the school setting.

29	4.36	4.14	The feeling that people care about each other is present in the school.
30	4.82	4.31	The physical condition of the school facility is acceptable.
31	3.64	2.84	People at this school complain a lot.
40	4.79	2.89	Faculty and staff morale at this school is low.
41	4.64	4.27	Teachers are sensitive and responsive to the needs of students.
45	4.36	3.46	The administration is sensitive and responsive to the needs of teachers.
46	4.55	2.81	The administration shows favoritism to some constituents.
47	4.27	3.57	There is a feeling of togetherness/community at this school.

Sense of Mission: The degree to which the faculty agrees on a philosophy of education and is committed to the school's goals and objectives.

32	4.68	4.62	The school's mission is posted for everyone to see.
33	4.50	3.81	A short phrase that captures the school's mission has been developed and placed in conspicuous places, for example, on stationery, buses, etc.
34	4.50	4.22	The administration creates opportunities for the mission/vision to be shared with constituents.
35	4.77	4.62	The faculty was involved in creating the mission.
36	4.77	4.24	A mission statement has been created, but it is not seen or shared.
37	4.55	4.41	The faculty is in agreement as to the mission of the school.

| 38 | 4.77 | 4.11 | The mission statement is of little value for what happens at our school. |
| 39 | 4.50 | 3.65 | If asked, the faculty are able to describe the school's mission statement. |

Parent Involvement: The administration has created an environment that encourages parents to be involved.

42	4.50	3.76	Parents are recruited to serve as volunteers at the school.
43	4.27	3.97	The administration supports some form of media (newsletter, computer, etc.) to communicate with constituents on a regular basis.
44	4.41	3.86	The relationship that exists between parents and the teachers is a good one.
52	4.09	3.78	The relationship that exists between parents and the administration is a good one.
53	4.59	4.16	It is easy for parents to find out how their child(ren) is/are doing academically.
60	4.45	3.95	It is easy for parents to find out what their child(ren) must do for homework.
61	4.73	4.22	The administration has recruited business/community partners.
62	4.45	3.76	Volunteers who participate at the school are recognized for their efforts.

Teaching: The degree to which teachers use appropriate instructional strategies to promote student achievement.

54	4.59	4.32	Teachers vary their instructional strategies according to the needs of the students.
55	4.55	4.24	The behavior of the teachers communicates that they care about their students.
58	4.45	3.86	Homework assignments are appropriate for the student and subject.
59	4.59	3.86	Teachers explain the objective(s) of the activity or lesson for the day.
71	2.68	3.67	Teachers at this school are unable to control students in their classroom.
72	4.36	4.03	Teachers motivate the students to want to learn.
77	4.27	4.03	Teachers review previous work before introducing new material.

| 78 | 4.64 | 4.19 | Teachers help students to feel good about themselves. |

Discipline: The degree to which the administration and teachers are able to control the behavior of the students.

65	4.55	4.35	The atmosphere in the classroom is conducive to learning.
66	4.24	2.76	The procedure the administration has in place for office referrals and discipline is effective.
67	4.32	2.95	The degree of communication with teachers about an office referral is appropriate.
73	4.50	4.05	Students' safety is a problem at this school.
74	4.09	3.27	The administration supports teachers in matters related to student discipline.
82	4.18	3.65	The responsibility for student behavior is shared by staff/faculty members.
83	4.18	3.65	Communication with parents about student misbehavior is appropriate.
84	3.95	3.35	The administrative plan for dealing with student absences and tardies is appropriate.

Assessment/Time on Task: What the teachers and administration do to monitor student achievement and time on task.

68	4.55	3.76	Student achievement data are monitored by the administration.
69	4.50	3.68	Student achievement data are used to provide feedback to teachers.
70	4.36	3.62	Student achievement data are used to evaluate the effectiveness of a program or change in the curriculum.
75	4.55	4.11	Teachers' grading practices are based on a variety of activities that monitor student learning.
76	4.41	4.11	Classroom instruction starts and ends on time.
88	4.41	3.95	The administration does their best to minimize time lost due to pull out programs and/or extra-curricular activities.
89	4.36	4.14	The administration does their best to minimize time lost due to classroom interruptions.
90	4.23	3.81	Teachers' classroom management practices are effective in keeping students on task.

Instructional Leadership: What the administration does to improve student achievement.

79	4.27	3.57	The amount and type of feedback the administration gives teachers is appropriate.
80	4.55	4.00	The administration makes sure that teachers have adequate materials and supplies.
81	4.27	3.78	The principal spends too much time in the office.
91	4.41	4.05	The administration uses staff development plans to promote student achievement.
92	4.55	4.30	The administration provides opportunities for teachers to grow professionally.
93	3.95	3.76	The administration empowers the faculty and staff.
97	4.27	3.59	The principal organizes and plans so that things run smoothly.
98	4.41	3.41	The administration knows what is happening in the classroom.

Expectations: Those teacher and administrator behaviors that tell students what is expected.

85	4.32	3.89	Teachers make an effort to motivate those students who have low interest in schoolwork.
86	4.50	4.32	Teachers believe that every student can learn and improve.
87	4.45	4.22	The administration has high expectations for teacher performance.
94	4.59	4.05	The teachers have high expectations for student performance.
95	4.41	4.14	Students are given opportunities to show that they are responsible.
96	4.36	4.05	Teachers stress continuity of learning and make connections between subject matter taught.
99	4.36	3.84	Teachers place too much emphasis on rote learning.
100	4.55	4.03	The use of workbooks, worksheets, and other fill-in-the-blank-type materials is excessive.

Appendix E

Character Elementary School

Spring 2015

SELECTED CHARACTER TRAITS AND THEIR CORRESPONDING BEHAVIORS

Mean Scores		Character Behaviors
2014	2015	Respect for self/Others/Property
3.02	3.20	Students think about the feelings of other students.
3.29	3.83	Students take care of school property.
3.82	3.88	Students like themselves.
2.91	3.16	Students make school property look better.
3.42	3.82	Students do things that hurt other students.
3.50	3.97	Students do things that are not good for themselves.
3.53	3.44	Students believe that keeping your body clean is important
3.87	3.74	Students use tobacco.
3.67	3.36	Students use drugs and/or alcohol
		Honesty
2.75	3.25	Students think it is okay to do something as long as they don't get caught.
3.79	4.17	Students take things that don't belong to them.
3.19	3.58	Students turn in money or things that have been lost, if they find them.
2.91	3.29	Students tell the truth.
3.26	3.59	Students can be trusted.

Self-control/Discipline

3.03	3.46	Students control themselves/behave, when they feel the need to.
3.53	3.66	Students do what the teachers ask them to do.
3.11	3.49	Students stay away from things that are not good for them or that will get them into trouble.
2.98	3.31	Students are able to wait to get what they want.
3.19	3.40	Students pay attention in class.
<u>3.74</u>	<u>3.91</u>	<u>Students let other students tell them what to do.</u>
2.96	3.37	Students control their anger.

Responsibility/Dependability/Accountability

3.21	3.46	Students can be trusted to do what they say they will do.
<u>2.83</u>	<u>3.09</u>	<u>Students make excuses or argue about the consequences when they get in trouble.</u>
3.10	3.23	Students do what the teacher asks without having to be reminded.
3.10	3.27	Students complete their class work on time.
3.11	3.28	Students turn in their homework on time.
3.04	3.32	Students accept the consequences of their decisions/actions.

Integrity/Fairness

<u>2.45</u>	<u>2.68</u>	<u>Students go along with the most popular students instead of those who are not popular.</u>
3.27	3.48	Students do what they are supposed to do.
<u>3.56</u>	<u>3.63</u>	<u>Students let other students talk them into doing something that is wrong.</u>
<u>3.17</u>	<u>3.43</u>	<u>Students take advantage of other students, if given the chance.</u>
<u>2.94</u>	<u>3.33</u>	<u>Students treat others the way they would want to be treated.</u>
<u>3.14</u>	<u>3.16</u>	<u>Students stand up or speak out for what they believe is right.</u>

Perseverance/Diligence

3.44	3.57	Students try hard when faced with a problem.
2.83	3.16	Students think about and plan their work.
<u>3.44</u>	<u>3.52</u>	<u>Students give up when they fail or do not succeed.</u>
3.02	3.35	Students finish an assignment, no matter how long it takes.
<u>3.03</u>	<u>3.17</u>	<u>Students have trouble keeping their thoughts on their work.</u>

2.98	3.33	<u>Students daydream, doodle, stare out of the window.</u>

Cooperation

3.42	3.59	Students help each other.
3.68	3.66	Students help the teacher.
<u>3.36</u>	<u>3.64</u>	<u>Students fight with each other.</u>
3.14	3.49	Students work well in groups.
<u>3.21</u>	<u>3.24</u>	<u>Students argue with each other.</u>
2.96	3.18	Students compromise to solve a conflict/problem.

Compassion/Empathy

3.13	2.98	Students feel sorry for students who are having a problem.
<u>3.05</u>	<u>2.98</u>	<u>Students pick on each other.</u>
<u>3.31</u>	<u>3.08</u>	<u>Students say/do things that hurt other students.</u>
2.90	2.72	Students help another student, who is being picked on.
3.18	3.01	Students listen to each other's problems.
3.10	3.00	Students comfort/console other students, who have a problem.

Kindness

3.30	3.48	Students are nice to each other.
3.46	3.67	Students are nice to teachers and other adults.
<u>3.18</u>	<u>3.37</u>	<u>Students say things about others that are harmful.</u>
3.12	3.45	Students give compliments to each other.
<u>3.42</u>	<u>3.56</u>	<u>Students are cruel to each other.</u>
3.23	3.38	Students help students who have physical or mental disabilities.

Forgiveness

<u>2.86</u>	<u>3.04</u>	<u>Students try to get even.</u>
2.91	3.16	Students accept the mistakes of others.
<u>2.95</u>	<u>3.10</u>	<u>Students are mean to someone because of something that person did to them in the past.</u>
3.16	3.56	Students accept an apology to end a problem.

Patriotism/Citizenship

3.62	3.76	Students are positive about their country.
3.54	3.57	Students are positive about the police.
3.27	3.58	Students are positive about the need for rules and laws.

3.35	3.40	Students care about their community.
3.28	3.61	Students care about their school.
3.10	3.29	Students volunteer their services to help where needed.

Tolerance/Diversity

3.79	3.98	Students accept students who are of different religion.
3.12	3.22	Students make fun of ideas that are different from theirs.
3.10	3.53	Students accept differences of opinion.
3.27	3.44	Students make fun of students who are different.
3.61	3.53	Students accept students who are from a different race.
3.03	3.50	Students make an effort to understand students who are different.

Courtesy/Politeness

2.91	3.08	Students interrupt when others are talking.
3.17	3.35	Students use curse words or "bad language."
2.97	3.21	Students call each other names.
3.01	3.40	Students say things, like, "Thank you," "Pardon me," etc. when appropriate.
3.20	3.28	Students listen when someone is talking to them.
2.97	3.17	Students ignore other students.
3.31	3.42	Students talk back to teachers and other adults.

Generosity/Charity

3.06	2.96	Students are more concerned about themselves than they are of others.
3.13	3.18	Students want to help the less fortunate.
3.08	3.05	Students are willing to share what they have with others.
2.81	2.95	Students want to know what is in "it" for themselves.

Sportsmanship

2.88	2.97	Students become angry when they lose.
3.12	3.38	Students congratulate their opponents, whether they win or lose.
2.96	3.16	Students quit trying, if they know that they are going to lose.
3.09	3.33	Students will cheat to win.
2.84	3.11	Students agree that, "How the game is played," is more important than winning.

Humility

		Students care too much about their appearance, for
2.58	2.88	example, having the right clothing, looking just right, etc.
2.80	3.09	Students brag about themselves.
2.67	2.81	Students want to be the center of attention.
3.23	3.23	Students put down other students.
2.86	3.24	Students act as if they are better than other students
3.09	3.37	Students admit when they are wrong.

About the Authors

Cletus R. Bulach is associate professor emeritus at the University of West Georgia and the CEO of the Professional Development and Assessment Center. The center provides training to improve leadership skills in human relations, conflict management, and group management. He has developed surveys to collect data on school climate and culture, leadership behavior, teacher-caring behaviors, bullying behavior, character-related behavior, and levels of openness and trust. Manuscripts that describe research conducted with these data collection surveys can be found on his website at www.westga.edu/~cbulach. His many publications include 37 citations in the ERIC data base. Prior to forming the consulting agency and retiring from the professoriate in 2003, he served as a superintendent (14 years), school administrator, and teacher in Ohio and retired after 30 years' service in 1990.

Fred C. Lunenburg is the Jimmy N. Merchant Professor of Education at Sam Houston State University, where he teaches courses in educational leadership. He has taught at the University of Louisville and Loyola University Chicago. In addition, he has served as an English teacher and reading specialist, principal, superintendent of schools, and university dean. He has authored or co-authored 26 books and more than 200 journal articles.

Les Potter is the director of American International School West in Cairo, Egypt. Prior to that he was an associate professor and the academic chair of the College of Education at Daytona State College, Daytona Beach, Florida. Les has been principal of four high schools and three middle schools in four states. He was selected Principal of the Year for both South Carolina and North Carolina. He has had various roles in education during his 41+ years in public education. Additionally, Les has been a tenure track professor in educational leadership and foundations at the University of South Alabama and the University of West Georgia. Les has over 90 books, chapters, book reviews, and articles published in numerous educational journals. He is a reviewer and editor for *Eye on Education* and *Education Digest*.